COURTESY DENVER ART MUSEUM

The Crazy Quilt Handbook
by Judith Montano

C&T Publishing, P.O. Box 1456, Lafayette, CA 94549

Other Fine Quilting Books from C&T Publishing

An Amish Adventure
Roberta Horton

Memorabilia Quilting
Jean Wells

Heirloom Machine Quilting
Harriet Hargrave

Picture This
Jean Wells and Marina Anderson

Friendship's Offering
Susan McKelvey

A Celebration of Hearts
Jean Wells and Marina Anderson

Landscapes & Illusions
Joen Wolfrom

Plaids and Stripes
Roberta Horton

Mastering Machine Appliqué
Harriet Hargrave

Story Quilts
Mary Mashuta

Quilting Designs from the Amish
Pepper Cory

Wearable Art for Real People
Mary Mashuta

For a complete listing of books, write for a free catalog from:
C&T Publishing
P.O. Box 1456
Lafayette, CA 94549

© 1986 by Judith Montano

Edited and Designed by Patricia Wilens

Illustrations by Ann Davis Nunemacher

Published by C&T Publishing
P.O. Box 1456, Lafayette, CA 94549

ISBN 0-914881-05-1

Library of Congress Catalog Card No.: 86-71560

Printed in the United States of America

20 19 18 17 16 15 14 13 12 11

TABLE OF CONTENTS

Dedication
For Fred, Jason and Madeleine
My special family, who go beyond the call of duty
by living with a "creative" person

ABOUT THE AUTHOR

Judith Montano is a Canadian-born artist following a family tradition of quilting and crafts. She incorporates ethnic influences from world travels into her work, as well as her love of the land and memories of her Alberta ranch home.

Judith started quilting when her family was living in Houston, Texas, where she was an active member of the Kingwood Quilt Guild. Her first prize winning quilt was made in 1980, when she won Best of Show at the Calgary Exhibition and Stampede in Calgary, Alberta, Canada. It was a special victory, because her great-grandmother won the same award in 1934.

Crazy quilting is a constant form of expression for Judith. She has evolved it into a contemporary style and has created pictoral quilts and art garments with Victorian stitches, beading and punchneedle embroidery. Her garments and quilts have won several design awards in Canada and the U.S. and have been pictured in several national magazines.

Judith is a graduate of the University of California at Chico, and holds a degree in art and journalism. She enjoys teaching and lecturing, as well as commission work in her home studio. She is a part-time staff aide in the textile department of the Denver Art Museum.

Judith's family includes her husband, Fred, and their children Jason and Madeleine. The Montanos live near Castle Rock, Colorado.

ACKNOWLEDGEMENTS & THANKS

This book is the result of many years of study and work. It could never have come about without the support of family and friends. I want to give a special thank you to my husband, Fred, who is always there for encouragement and help; to my son, Jason, who dares to be a dreamer and is too much like his mother; to my daughter, Madeleine, who is my sweet, dear friend and lover of animals and people.

A very grateful thank you to my parents, Allen and Joyce, and to my godparents, Uncle Harry and Aunt Muriel. Together, the four of them gave me a wonderful heritage.

A special thank you to my cousin, Francis Lange, who drops everything to model my art garments.

I am lucky to have many supportive and interesting friends. Without them, I would probably not have written this book. I would like to thank Marinda Brown-Stewart, Priscilla Miller, Donna Wilder, Imelda DeGraw, Margaret Dittman, Alice Bertling, Juanita Ely, Pat Rogers, Carol Moderi, Chris Nyberg, Bill Lober and Heidi Schrader Harrison.

Outdoor photography was shot at the Denver Botanic Gardens and at the Montano home.

A word of grateful acknowledgement goes to the Denver Art Museum and its staff for the museum's support of this project and for graciously allowing us to photograph antique quilts from its wonderful collection. Photos of quilt details are all from D.A.M. quilts.

Crazy Quilt Definitions

Crazy quilting can be defined as a method of laying down bits and pieces of fabric in a haphazard fashion and sewing or appliqueing them to a whole cloth. After the whole cloth is completely covered, each seam is covered with decorative details and embroidery stitches.

Judith Montano, 1986

A patchwork quilt without ordered design

Webster's Seventh
New Collegiate Dictionary

. . . Into them women stitched their longings — their hunger for beauty, their impatience with the monotony of their days, their desire for change or adventure, their love for color, which common custom said they might not display in dress. And in the thrill of creating new colors and designing new patterns, daring with cloth and needle to do what someone else had not done, the art of quiltmaking . . . caused much excitement of fancy in days that would otherwise have been uneventful.

Henderson McDermott
The Farm Journal, circa 1930

Out in the Open: *Confessions of a Crazy Quilter*

Crazy quilts have always fascinated me. Though other crafts may distract me, I am always drawn back to these beautiful, outrageous crazy quilts. They remind me of mysterious, glittering jewels, like gypsy cousins peeking out from a patchwork of traditional sister quilts. They seem like wild, black sheep children, tolerated by conservative relatives.

Crazy quilting is a special love of mine, the answer to all my diverse pleasures. What other handcraft combines embroidery, sewing, applique, laces, ribbons, buttons, beading, painting and color design?

My determination to make crazy quilts began soon after I was married, when we lived in Europe. In England, I saw some beautiful Victorian crazy quilts at a museum. They really sparked my interest and I looked about for information on how to make them, but nothing seemed available. Meanwhile, I turned to traditional quilting. I had an excellent teacher and made several nice quilts, but I never lost the longing to make a crazy quilt.

Finally, I decided to teach myself. If our forebears could make crazy quilts, so could I. Because I couldn't find how-to information and because crazy quilts were not popular then, I kept very quiet about it. I've kept my first attempt as a lesson in humility.

I worked for 10 years without guidance. Through trial and error, I learned what works, shortcuts, etc. I learned the Victorian stitches from an embroidery book. It was many years, though, before I was invited to share my findings by teaching a class in crazy quilting. I gave my first class in the late '70s and only three people showed up. Today, though, my classes are filled and people are interested in learning to make crazy quilts. The crazy quilt has been accepted . . . again.

Links with the Past

I believe that one's background and upbringing preface our special interests. The texture of my background has a lot to do with my love for crazy quilting. I was raised on a cattle ranch in Alberta, Canada, right at the base of the Rocky Mountains. Our ranch, the Bar U, was quite isolated. Fortunately, my mother is a multi-talented woman, excelling at needlework, pottery, music and art. She employed her skills to keep us children busy and amused, and she taught me needlework at an early age.

Among our neighbors were an Indian reserve and a Hutterite colony. (Hutterites are similar to the Amish, but they live in communes and use mechanized farm machinery.) As a girl, I loved to visit these distant neighbors with my father.

From my Stoney Indian friends, I developed a love for rich, vivid colors and beads. From my Hutterite friends, I enriched my admiration for embroidery and needlework. Above all, from my father, I developed a great love for the land and the ranching life. It was my greatest joy to be his right-hand cowgirl. Some of my dearest memories are of riding with him over the beautiful, wild foothills of Alberta. Many of those Alberta sunsets find their way into my crazy quilting today.

Crazy quilting is part of my heritage, too, handed down from my grandmother. A few years ago, in a chest filled with handiwork of Grandmother Baker's, my aunt showed me a lovely crazy quilt tucked away with the tablecloths. It is a wonderful link with the past and my own passion for crazy quilting. That quilt is a spiritual bond between me and my grandmother.

Trailblazers

During the years I worked along in my studio, crazy quilting everything I could think of, three trailblazers helped bring crazy quilting back to the public's attention. One is Dixie Haywood, who specializes in machine crazy quilting and has published books on this subject. Another is Dorothy Bond, who has printed a delightful book on Victorian stitches. The third is Penny McMorris, author of a wonderful book on historical aspects of crazy quilting. She is greatly responsible for the current interest.

Now I hope to provide you with a how-to book that touches on the history, stitches, embellishments and contemporary applications of crazy quilting, as well as my original designs. My goal is to open the door to an old but new and exciting interest, to bring crazy quilting out into the open for today's crafters.

Historical Perspective: *The Crazy Quilt Legacy*

Crazy quilts are fabric documentations of history. We can stand in front of an old crazy quilt and see what life was like when the quilt was made. Bits of local and national history combine to give us an overall impression of nineteenth century life and customs. Lush velvets, satins and rich silks mix with colorful, glazed chintz and cottons. In a crazy quilt, we can see the fabrics of life — those that were used every day and those that were worn only for special occasions. In their hodge-podge way, Victorian crazy quilts are a reflection of the fashions and fads of their time.

The Victorian era officially dates from 1837 to 1901, the reign of Britain's Queen Victoria, who gave her name to an age. It was a time when Great Britain was the most powerful nation on earth, with dominions on every continent, and her influence was widespread. Victoria (and her extensive family) dominated the fashion of the times.

Victoria spent much of her life in an overdone, maudlin state of widowhood. She collected endless mementos, particularly of her dear departed Albert, until she lived amid a virtual chaos of memorabilia. It finally reached the point at which the Queen, after dinner, held court in the corridors of Windsor Castle because her rooms were too crowded to admit her assembled attendants.

This fussiness was reflected in the fashions of dress and decorating. Women wore tight bodices over huge hoop skirts, topped in the back by ridiculous bustles. Ribbons, laces and ruffles appeared in profusion. At home, too, more was better and the best decorators strove to emulate the Queen's clutter.

Crazy quilts were a natural outgrowth of the environment, since needlework was one of a very few "acceptable" occupations for women. Crazy quilts combined opulent colors, lush fabrics and unrestrained pattern. They also served the sentimental by becoming depositories of all sorts of memorabilia. Other influences of fashion are also evident.

Some people question whether the crazy quilt dates from the Victorian era or whether it is older, indeed the oldest of American quilts. I believe it must be credited to the Victorians. We know the practical, hard-working pioneer woman "discovered" pieced quilts, salvaging every precious bit of cloth to make into bed cover-ings. Quilted or tied, these were strictly for utility, for the pioneers had no time or materials for frivolous decoration. Crazy quilts require a lot of fabric, especially for base and backing. They are usually not very practical, since they are more decorative than warm.

The crazy quilt's heyday was after the Civil War, when the nation came of age and more women had the time and money to devote to sewing for pleasure. Especially in big cities, decorative art became the rage and every woman strove to create a beautiful home. Crazy quilts fit right in with the idea that more was better.

The Centennial Exposition of 1876 is a watermark in the development of crazy quilting in the U.S. Held in Philadelphia, many countries set up elaborate exhibits. The most popular was the Japanese pavilion and, suddenly, anything of Japanese design was all the rage. Like wallpaper and fabrics, embroidery books were printed with Oriental designs and these soon appeared in profusion on crazy quilts. Japanese favored asymmetrical design and this, too, was reflected in the quilts.

Detail from antique quilt pictured on Page 5. This oriental teapot, worked in outline, is typical of the Japanese designs that became popular embroidery motifs following the Centennial Exposition of 1876.

Several historians claim the crazy quilt originated with a single Japanese picture, that it was an attempt to copy the crazed pavement in a Japanese panel. Others say the Japanese "cracked ice" china design that became popular at this time was the inspiration. However it came about, Japanese influence is evident in many antique crazy quilts.

For the last quarter of the nineteenth century, crazy quilting was definitely the "in" thing to do. Every woman *had* to have a crazy quilt. The more intricate and busy it was, the better.

Crazy quilting was a blessing to a number of manufacturers, who encouraged its popularity. Crazy quilting might be one of the first national fads fanned by commercial interests. Silk makers were delighted with the trend and cashed in by selling pattern books, packets of silk scraps, silk thread and metallics. Women's magazines

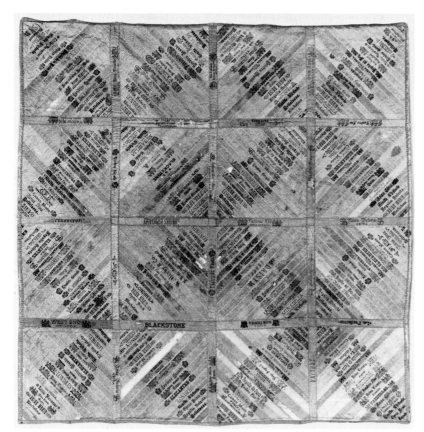

This piece is made entirely of yellow cigar silk ribbons, sewn into squares and set together like a Log Cabin "Barn Raising" into a throw approximately 37" square. Silks were offered as premiums in boxes of cigars, and many Victorian ladies had large ribbon collections. The throw was made between 1875 and 1900. (Courtesy D.A.M.)

This detail of the Wall Hanging project (pictured on Page 33) shows how cigarette silks can be used in contemporary work. Cigarette silks were prints, depicting animals, flags and famous persons of the time, that were tucked inside cigarette packets. They were collected and used widely by Victorian quilters. The author found 40 silks, mostly from Turkey Red and Egyptienne brands, in an antique shop, sewn to a muslin base. The piece on the front cover features a cigarette silk.

These details, taken from different quilts, show the popularity of Kate Greenaway designs in Victorian crazy quilts. Above is a printed ribbon from one quilt; below is the same design, copied in outline embroidery. Miss Greenaway (1846-1901) was a popular English painter & illustrator, best known for drawings of children. Courtesy D.A.M.

were full of advice on making crazy quilts, as well as the arts of homemaking. The Victorians respected handiwork and endorsed the motto, "Happy hands are busy hands."

Peeking out from among the fabric pieces are wonderful silk premium ribbons. These small rectangular ribbons were give-aways, tucked into cigarette packets and cigar boxes by the manufacturer. The ribbons featured celebrities of the era — actors, opera stars and politicians — as well as animals, national flags, Indians, royalty and city flags. Luckily, the crazy quilt makers prized these ribbons and many were woven into their quilts to tell us about Victorian life.

Also highlighting some of the fabrics are small, intricate oil paintings. Some of these depict flowers, animals and Kate Greenaway children. Many original paintings represent family members and pets, but most of these designs were taken from pattern books.

The most common embellishment technique was embroidery. Animals, birds, children and flowers were favorite Victorian motifs, as were Japanese designs. Many designs were taken from patterns that were perforated so the motif could be outlined on the fabric with a white powder. With a sharp needle, a picture magazine and a stamping pad filled with powder, a crazy quilter could make any kind of embroidery design.

Remember that a special function of these quilts was to serve as a personal scrapbook. Important dates are often embroidered, as are the initials of the maker or of loved ones. Birthdays, weddings and deaths are commemorated in lovely italicized embroideries. Mementos of special occasions decorate the quilts, with bits of clothing fabrics and handkerchiefs incorporated into the fabrics.

Most Victorian crazy quilts were made as a throw; that is, a much smaller size than a bed quilt. They were most often on display in the parlor, thrown over the back of the sofa or draped over the piano. Sometimes they were displayed on the wall. As a throw, the quilt could be used for afternoon naps or for a lap throw on a nippy day when visitors came to call.

If they were used on beds at all, the crazy quilt was often the best quilt, taken out only for special occasions and only for the guest of honor.

Crazy quilting also was used for smaller items. Pillows and table runners were popular and added greatly to the parlor decor. Many were framed with velvet borders and silk ruffles, or highlighted with borders of elaborate crochet. Pianos were a fixture of a well furnished Victorian home and a piano scarf was often an ideal showcase for crazy quilting.

Farm and country women were at a bit of a disadvantage, as they did not have easy access to silks and other fancy fabrics. Their crazy quilts were made mostly of wool, cottons and a few special fabrics.

Farm women worked like men in the fields, but still found time for needlework. Their crazy quilts are a tribute to every woman's basic need to beautify her surroundings. My grandmother's quilt reflects the country woman's point of view. A farm wife, she made the quilt in 1932 and it took many long evenings to complete. Her name was Bessie Burns Baker and she loved needlework. Her own mother was a master quilter. Though she worked hard all day, my father and his sister remember her working by lamplight over her quilt. (See photo, Page 22.) My grandparents emigrated from Oklahoma and Kansas to take up farming near Cayley, Alberta, Canada. We can only imagine the long, hard hours and the loneliness.

9A. This quilt was made in 1879 by Addie Julia Bertschy Adams (1858-1945). The patches of velvet, plush, satins and silks are highly decorated with elaborate embroideries. The deep red velvet border has been patched with sections of blue. It is initialed in several places and the date, Aug. 27, 1879, appears at the bottom, center.

9B. Souvenir ribbons of campaigns and special events were often sewn into crazy quilts. This one, from a quilt made in the 1890's, preserves fond memories of a local lodge dance.

Contemporary Crazy Quilting

Just as in Victorian times, we can use crazy quilting in our lives today. Our philosophies of fashion and interior design are very flexible and we can live with whatever pleases us.

Interior Design & Accessories

The country look that swept the 1980's has introduced a slightly cluttered look in many homes, reminiscent of Victorian days. It is quite fashionable now to mix old with new, pattern on pattern and a whole palette of colors. Crazy quilting fits right in.

There's no reason why crazy quilting can't fit a contemporary setting, too. By using all solid colors and relatively larger shapes, a crazy quilt can be very sophisticated. A good idea is to vary the size and shape, in this case. Instead of a traditional square, the quilt can be a rectangular banner, hung above eye level.

Pillows are a fast and easy way to make a decorative statement. Crazy quilting makes effective pillows in heart, fan and round shapes that make terrific sofa accents. Placemats can be made fast and easy with washable cottons (be sure they're prewashed). A good blend of fabrics and colors make a versatile table setting.

Let your imagination guide you in decorating with crazy quilting. It can be a dramatic focus of a room or a special, colorful accent.

Family Heirlooms and Momentos

Crazy quilting is a special way to commemorate important occasions. By using significant fabrics and lace, and adding special dates and initials, a framed fabric picture can become a family treasure. Keep this in mind for a new baby or family anniversary.

A wall hanging fits any decor and can be the collection point for family momentos. Use handkerchiefs, laces, hair ribbons, fabrics from special garments and fabric painting to create a unique family tribute.

Friendship Quilts

The crazy quilt is a perfect vehicle for a group effort such as a friendship quilt. Forty friends in my Texas quilt guild contributed to a surprise going-away gift for me that kept me busy and happy assembling the donated pieces in my new home. We all shared the pleasure when it won Judges Choice at the Colorado State Fair. (See Kingwood Quilt, back cover.) The ease of incorporating little pieces of special things, dates and initials and assembling assorted shapes and sizes of the contributions make a crazy quilt an ideal project for guilds and church groups.

Jewelry and Clothing

Not all of us have time to make quilts, but we can work crazy quilting into smaller projects such as clothing and soft sculptured jewelry. This cluttered but elegant look makes wonderful pendants and collars. Pendants can be made in any shape or size if you use my special method of putting pendants together (see project instructions, Page 46). Crazy quilt jewelry is not only wonderful to wear, but it makes a very personal gift, too. Just remember to keep the fabric pieces proportionately small — a 4″ pendant is much more effective with small, irregular shapes than just two or three pieces of fabric.

There are several popular books devoted to personalized clothing and patterns that adapt well to special techniques. The versatility of crazy quilting allows you to personalize a garment for your mood or lifestyle. Colors can be vibrant or subdued, fabrics can be glitzy or soft, sophisticated and elegant or country and homespun.

With our easy access to all kinds of fabrics and threads, it seems right that crazy quilting should take its place in the evolution of contemporary quilting. It lets us show off our needlework, document our way of life and, above all, preserve our family histories and traditions.

Printed silks, like this one from an antique Victorian quilt, were quick and easy ways to achieve a pictoral effect. Any fabric print, appliqued onto a fabric base and edged with embroidery stitches, can be used this way.

Some of the fabrics in my grandmother's quilt are disintegrating, but it still has a story to tell. Past memories and future hopes are woven into this quilt. It includes pieces of her dresses, suiting from my grandfather's best suit and shirting from those he wore in the fields. One piece is from a baby dress that belonged to little Agnes, their first daughter who died at age five. A special handkerchief, brought back from the Great War by an uncle, is proudly displayed.

This crazy quilt is not as lush or fancy as other crazy quilts, but it is just as much a document of history, a tribute to a young farm wife who labored to create something beautiful for her home.

If you are interested in knowing more about the history of crazy quilts, I recommend Crazy Quilts by Penny McMorris (see bibliography). It is a very concise and detailed book with many beautiful photographs of antique quilts.

Design Elements for Successful Crazy Quilting

There are five basic elements in the recipe for successful crazy quilting. By using the right mix of color, repetition, balance, fabrics (solids and patterns) and embellishment, you will be happy with the result. The ideas discussed here relate to virtually any project, regardless of size or intended use. I will often refer to a vest as an example, but the same principles apply to full size quilts, framed pictures, etc., as well as to garments.

Because so many people like to embellish clothing with crazy quilting, let's begin with a brief look at garment patterns.

Adapting Crazy Quilting to Garment Patterns

Selecting Patterns

Choose patterns that have flat areas for embellishment or high interest areas, such as borders or a yoke, that will showcase crazy quilting. Many of the ethnic or period pattern designs available are perfect for crazy quilting.

The lines of the garment should be simple so as not to compete with the crazy quilting. Darts pose an obvious problem but they are not impossible.

When you find a suitable pattern, it is best to buy it right away. Pattern companies are constantly changing their lines and you can't depend on the pattern being available in the future. If you want to make garments for friends and relatives, buy a variety of sizes in a pattern that you feel is universal. Purchase the usual pattern size; crazy quilting does not affect the fit of the garment.

Begin With A Bigger Base

Work with a foundation that is larger than the actual pattern. For example, if I am going to crazy quilt the yoke of a vest or blouse, I transfer the yoke outline onto a base of muslin or cotton outing. On this foundation, I draw the actual seam lines, but I cut out the shape

2″ larger all around. This allows for shrinkage that may occur with piecing. Outside the confines of the seam lines, I may leave the edges of the piecing unfinished since they are trimmed off later. This is a principle I use in all crazy quilting; whether the piece is to be a dress, a pillow or a pendant, I always sew the pieces down to a base that is cut larger than desired finished size.

Design Placement

Often you will see a garment that has obviously taken many hours to produce, but it somehow doesn't look right and isn't very flattering. Yet, with all that time and effort, it *ought* to be gorgeous.

Maybe the stitcher has produced a folded star vest. The colors are lovely and she's very proud of it. But where is the star? Smack dab in the middle of her back, it is the perfect target for a passing archer! Perhaps the same stitcher makes a folded star jacket. It is very nice and the quilting is superb. Why does it remind us of a German opera star with an iron bra? Because the two stars are placed on either side of the jacket front, drawing unnecessary attention to her bosom.

Our proud stitcher, who has enough padding of her own, makes a warm winter jacket, using ultra-loft batting that makes her look twice as big. To top it off, she uses a bright, geometric quilt pattern, so the effect makes her look like a moving quilt. Perhaps her jacket is a virtuoso work of Seminole patchwork, but the horizontal bands around the bottom bring attention to her ample hips.

Ever seen a quilter walking around with her arms up in the air? It's because all her handwork wound up under the arms! Making artistic garments is hard enough but not to have the needlework show is a crime.

If it seems that I'm familiar with this unfortunate lady, it's because I've described myself. Unfortunately, I made all these mistakes and learned the hard way an important lesson: position the crazy quilting where it will be seen, but not in a place where the attention doesn't suit the wearer of the garment.

Try to have a center of interest in every garment. This is the first thing people see, the area that immediately demands attention. This isn't necessarily the center of the garment, or of you. It can be up on one shoulder, or down at the hem on one side. Everything then works out from this center of interest. Perhaps you want to focus on a special fabric or embroidery. If this is the case, be sure the rest of the crazy quilting is complimentary to it without overshadowing it.

COLOR

Use of color is a very personal choice and the most difficult one for many. The best inspiration for successful color combination is the world of nature. The colors in flowers and animals, sunrises and sunsets are beautiful examples of effective, varied combinations. The *Color Wheel* is often used to illustrate color combinations found in nature.

The Color Wheel

The wheel can help you understand the logistics of mixing color. Everything begins with three *primary* colors — red, yellow and blue. By mixing equal amounts, we create *secondary* colors — orange, green and violet (purple). *Tertiary* colors are made by mixing a primary and the secondary color next to it.

The excitement of color is making combinations that work. The wheel illustrates the four combinations most often found in nature. A *monochromatic* color scheme uses a single color, perhaps varied with tints and shades of that color. An *analogous* color scheme combines neighboring colors on the wheel, such as blue and blue-green or red and red-orange. *Complimentary* colors are opposite each other on the wheel, such as red and green or purple and yellow. A *triad* uses three colors spaced equidistant on the wheel, such as orange, purple and green.

Adding a *neutral* to any combination extends it without changing its basic effect. Neutrals are black, white, gray, beige, brown and tan. Think of these as extenders. When in doubt, throw in a neutral.

Intensity

Intensity is the brightness or dullness of a color. Any color is brightest in its natural state, closest to primary. To change the intensity, or make it duller, the color is mixed with its compliment. For example, if we have red and want to dull it, we mix it with green. To change the intensity of the blue, mix it with orange. By adding more and more orange, you eventually get rust. A color is dullest when mixed with an equal amount of the complimentary color.

Value

The *value* of any color is changed by adding white or black. Adding white lightens the color to a tint, while black darkens it to a shade. For example, pink and burgundy are light and dark values of red. When both white and black are added to the primary color, the result is a grayed color.

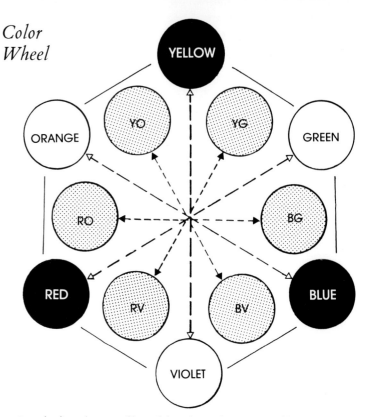

Color Wheel

A color's value is affected by the colors around it. In crazy quilting, the same fabric may read dark in one place and light in another, depending on the nature of its neighbors. A light fabric, surrounded by darker ones, seems to come forward; a dark fabric, surrounded by lighter ones, appears to recede.

Crazy quilting doesn't give you license to throw in *every* color, without rhyme or reason. Using the color wheel is a sure way to select an effective combination of colors. I like to use two dominant colors, with one or two neutrals. I choose various intensities and values of these colors, combining a good mix of prints, solids and textured fabrics.

Sort out the jumble of your fabrics and arrange them in color groups. Storing fabric this way makes color selection easier and more efficient. This way, you can reach for your stack or bundle of blues and find all the solids, textures and patterns in one place. Keep neutrals grouped together, too.

REPETITION AND BALANCE

Repetition and balance go hand in hand; we cannot have one without the other. Achieve a balance by repeating color, pattern and/or texture. To emphasize a particular shape or color, for example, you will achieve balance of design by repeating the shape (or color) throughout the work. Work out a sketch on paper before you begin to sew, so you get a visual idea of how the elements should repeat and balance one another.

If our example vest has a design on the back, try to have it fall over one shoulder. This offers a bit of a surprise, while following principles of repetition and balance. Repeating the design at the bottom of the other side adds to the overall effect.

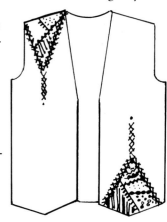

This fabric is dark when surrounded by light fabrics

The same fabric is light when surrounded by darker ones

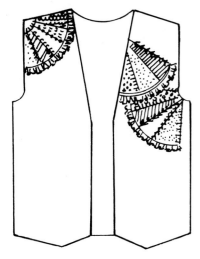

Perhaps the vest has crazy quilt fans on the front. To balance the design, have the fans spill over from side to the other. By repeating the fans over the surface of the vest, you will achieve a balanced design.

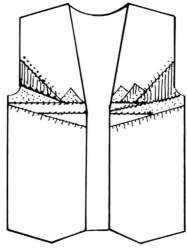

Color can be a unifying factor. If you want a "scenic" crazy quilt vest, draw the scene across the front and balance the design by carrying the color across both sides. Further balance is achieved by repeating stitches from side to side.

TEXTURE, PATTERNS & SOLIDS

In crazy quilting, it is very important to have a balance of texture and pattern. If you have too many busy prints, the work becomes a blur of confusion and the fancy stitches won't show up. It is important to bounce printed pieces off solids or textured fabrics. This adds interest and shows the pattern to best advantage. The same is true of textured fabrics. If your crazy quilt is made up only of textured fabrics, the texture is taken for granted and the quilt looks boring. Also, the fancy stitches get lost in the nap of some textures. In order for each fabric piece to harmonize with its neighbors, they must complement each other.

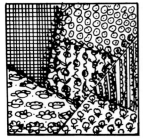

All pattern – loses the stitches

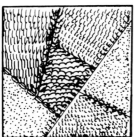

All texture – very boring; stitches tend to blend in and get lost

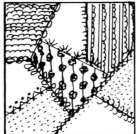

A balance of texture, solids and pattern

Fabrics in the texture category include satin, moire, wool, nubby fabrics, tweed, velvets or any fabric that has a special feel to it. Prints include any fabric that has a pattern, such as a pin dot, calico, decorator floral, cross hatching, even stripes.

Print fabric can have a large or small pattern, and it is important to select a pattern proportionate to the project. The larger the piece, the larger the print can be. With really large decorator prints, however, you can cut out just a portion of the design.

SELECTING FABRICS

One of the best things about crazy quilting is the infinite variety of fabrics it can employ. Virtually anything, from velvets to cottons, from lace to drapery fabric, can find its way into crazy quilting. Subsequently, the sources for fabric are equally varied.

Whereas solid fabrics are the foundation of crazy quilting, they can be mixed judiciously with patterns and textures. Solids are the base for embroidery and paintings and other details.

The most obvious source of fabric is the standard fabric store. There's one nearby just about anywhere. Here you can find satins, silks and wools. Dress weight velvets are great for many projects, especially cotton velveteen. Your best buys will be on the bargain tables; a ½ yard piece won't interest a dressmaker, but you can use it for many crazy quilt projects. Lace fabrics and sheers, with colored solids beneath them, might fit your project. Even plaids can be worked into crazy quilting.

A good source for cottons is the specialty quilt shop. Drapery shops are a good source of glazed chintz as well as moire and decorator cottons. Drapery moire is soft and manageable and has a better feel than most dress weights. If you buy lightweight drapery fabric, be sure it is pliable and will press into shape without creating a lumpy ridge in your work.

Before setting your heart on a particular fabric, consider its practicality. For some garments, you'll want washable fabric. Be sure these are preshrunk before you work with them. Fancier fabrics, such as satin, must be dry cleaned.

Because crazy quilting uses relatively small pieces, you can usually buy ½ yard lengths. If a piece is a large decorator print with lots of color and design, you might buy a yard or more. Neutral colors that you'll use again and again might be stored in longer lengths, too.

Old ties are a staple of second hand shops and garage sales and they are terrific for crazy quilting. They can be quite inexpensive and, since most are a synthetic weave, the reverse design is on the back and you get two design for the price. Ties are easy to pull apart and can be stored flat. Check out charity bazaars and garage sales everywhere you go and you'll soon have a superb tie collection.

All crazy quilting starts with a base or foundation, usually of preshrunk muslin or cotton outing. The foundation is always covered, front and back, so you can use up old fabric pieces for the foundation. You can get rid of real uglies this way! A base of cotton is particularly desirable for garments, because it drapes better than heavier fabrics. I use batting or fleece only for purses and small pendants.

Crazy Quilt How-To: *Laying the Foundation*

The great charm of crazy quilting is that there is no pattern. If you've selected your materials carefully, you've already laid the cornerstone of the finished piece. But how does that pile of fabric become a wonderful finished work? It is a process of evolution. As you sew, it will come to life under your hands. The pattern is your own individual interpretation.

You'll find what works best for you and for the particular project. Traditionalists may want to do all the sewing and needlework by hand. Personally, I feel the sewing machine is the most wonderful invention ever, and I use it as much as possible; the work goes much faster and leaves more time for embellishment.

Most piecing is done string quilting style, sewing each piece onto its neighbors. Curved edges are turned under to be appliqued later. It is not necessary to press each fabric before it is sewn because it will be heavily pressed afterwards. Press each seam line before the next piece is added.

Antique Method

In some Victorian crazy quilts, the edges of the individual piece were left unturned and tacked down only with the embroidery stitches. This was not very satisfactory, as the edges ravelled and did not stand up to use. Usually, edges were turned under and appliqued down.

Curved lines were thought to be more desirable than long, angular lines. Some Victorian pattern books suggested that larger pieces could be basted in place on the foundation and the smaller pieces fitted in.

The Victorians always sewed the fabric pieces to a foundation. Sometimes, the pieces were sewn onto a single large backing. More often, the work was done in small squares which were sewn together to make a large piece.

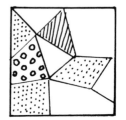

Antique Method — joined squares, hidden seams

Many stitchers did not like to see a line where the squares joined and would applique patches to cover seams. I use a similar method when I'm joining the pieces of a garment, the fronts and back of a vest, for example. At the side and shoulder seams, I leave the fabric at the outer edges hanging out over the seam line. When it's time to sew up the seam, I peel back the loose edges on one side, while the other side is trimmed even with the base. When the seams are sewn and the jagged edges are pressed flat, then the loose edges are appliqued onto the adjacent piece, completely hiding the seam line.

This technique applies to garments, of course, and can also be used for large quilts. Most projects, however, are better done on a one-piece foundation.

Contemporary Methods

There are two methods for sewing down fabrics to a foundation (which is cut 2″ larger than the desired finished size). On larger pieces, it is usually best to start in a corner and work outward in a fan-like progression. On smaller items, start with a center piece and work around it. We will go through each method step-by-step.

COURTESY DENVER ART MUSEUM

This crazy quilt is an example of a quilt made of assembled squares, with obvious seam lines. The quilt is a "country quilt", of wool and cotton. Feather stitch embroidery covers the seams. Made in Rexton, Kansas in 1910, the quilt measures 76″ × 69″.

Fan Style Method

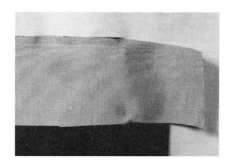

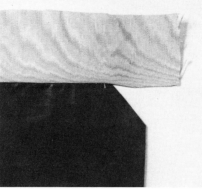

1. Cut a fabric piece with three or four angles. Pin it in place flush with the bottom left corner of the foundation fabric.

2. Select the next piece of fabric; cut it into a shape that complements the top edge of the corner piece. Lay it on the first angle, right sides of fabric together. Sew the two pieces together on this line using a ¼″ seam allowance. Flip the second piece over to the right side and press. If a tail of fabric hangs out, don't be concerned; it is dealt with later.

3. Cut pieces as you go. Don't worry if a piece seems too big for the spot you've selected; it can be trimmed after it is sewn down. Select the next fabric piece and lay it on the second angle of the corner piece, making sure it extends over both the previously sewn pieces. Sew it down as before. Trim away excess fabric, then flip it to the right side and press the seam flat.

4. Cover the third angle of the corner shape with the next shape in the same manner. Sew it down, flip it over and press.

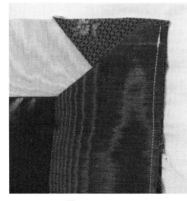

6. Fan back and forth, right to left, then left to right, until the foundation is completely filled. Always trim excess fabric from the seams; this will keep the work from bulking up.

5. Now you've completed the first clockwise level of the fan. Next, starting at the bottom of the last piece, you'll work counterclockwise to lay down the next level.

Center Piece Method

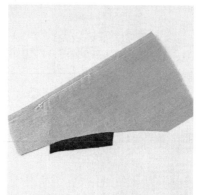

1. Cut a relatively small center piece from dark fabric. (A dark fabric is preferable because it recedes and brings the eye to center, a great base for embroidery.) Cut at least five angles on the center piece. Pin or baste it onto the foundation at the approximate center.

2. Cut the first shape and lay it against the first angle, right sides of fabric together. Sew a ¼" seam. Flip the shape over to the right side, then press the seam flat.

3. Cut a second shape and lay it along the next angle, working clockwise. Be sure the shape extends beyond the previous piece. Sew, then press the seam. Trim any excess fabric from the seam.

4. Continue around until all the angles of the center piece are stitched.

5. Continue working around, clockwise, until the whole foundation is filled. Keep a good balance of color, texture, pattern and solids as you work. Press all seams carefully. If you wish to use a fan, refer to the example on the previous page.

Once the base piece is complete, press it on both front and back. Trim all edges even with the foundation, unless you intend to join foundation pieces and want to hide the seams (see Antique Method, Page 14).

Problem Solving

As you work back and forth, you will sometimes find yourself in a spot you can't get out of. Here are some tips and suggestions for working your way out of a difficult spot.

Fans fill a V. Many beginners will find they have worked into a V angle that is difficult to sew into. If this happens, take advantage of it by sewing in a fan. Following the existing angle, just add long, narrow triangles until you work out of the V. The last side of the last triangle will have to be appliqued down.

Fans were a favorite Victorian motif and are very easy to make. They can be of irregular shape or very even, pointed or curved. A fan shape gives a sense of movement and can cover a large area. They are great corner fillers, too. A fan can be presewn and added to the foundation as a whole unit, or you can sew it in piece by piece as shown above.

Avoid inside angles. If you try to use a small piece of fabric that goes only halfway down an angle, you'll find yourself with a difficult inside angle. The only way to get out of this is to applique a small piece into the angle. It is easier to follow the whole angle as shown at left.

Prepieced strips fill in long lines. After you've added a few pieces, some of the lines may tend to get very long. This line can be shortened by cutting new angles from the long piece. Sometimes, I will create a long piece of fabric to fill the space by sewing several small pieces together, then sew them to the foundation as a unit. I will sew triangles, squares and rectangles together in a long wedge. Include curved edges, that have to be appliqued down anyway, on this long piece to help hide the long seam line.

Curves shorten lines. Long lines can be shortened with curved edges. Just about any curve must be hand appliqued onto its neighboring, after straight machine sewing is done.

Press under the seam allowance on the curved edge. Sew the straight edge of the piece onto the foundation, but leave the curved edge loose. Trace the curve onto the foundation, then flip the curved fabric back, out of the way of your sewing. Continue on with the crazy quilting, extending pieces just inside the traced curve. When the curved piece is smoothed down and appliqued in place, it will cover the raw edges. This works for both concave and convex shapes.

Decorative Details

For most people, this is the best part of crazy quilting, and the most creative. This is the process that turns an interesting work of piecing into something exotic and magical. When it comes to decorative detail, my motto is, "The more, the better."

Detail of Kingwood Quilt, pictured on back cover. A fabric painting of family pets, by Alice Bertling, highlights this section of the quilt. Just this small section offers many examples of other decorative detail techniques, including embroidery, beading, lacework, buttons, ribbons, ribbon roses and more.

Pictured opposite: *"Keeper of the Sacred Shield" is the title of this art garment, made of ultrasuede, cotton and silk. Crazy quilting is used to create mountains and hills, and every seam is covered with Victorian stitches and beads. This garment was made for the 1986 Statue of Liberty Fashion Show sponsored by Fairfield Processing Corp.*

I use less lace and ribbon on clothing, jewelry and purses, and never ruffles, because they add too much bulk to the figure. On these pieces, emphasize embroidery instead. Laces, bows and ruffles are fine for items such as wall hangings and pillows since they are not handled as much and can carry more frills.

Enhancements can be divided into those that are done before the base work and those done after. Enhancements done before sewing are the larger, more ambitious decorations such as embroidery pictures, calligraphy, painting and photo transfer. These are usually worked onto large pieces of fabric that can be trimmed and shaped to fit into the piecework as it evolves.

Once the foundation is complete, work in a set order of sequence — this saves much time and trouble from going back and forth. First, add the lace, ribbons and bows. Then, cover the remaining seams with embroidery. When all the embroidery is done, the beading is next. Add buttons last, as they are usually bulkiest.

We will look at each technique in turn, beginning with those enhancements generally done before the basework. Don't feel that you have to incorporate a little bit of everything; choose the decorative details that you like the most and that are most appropriate to your project.

EMBROIDERIES

Embroidery is an indispensable element of crazy quilting. The last chapter of this book features Victorian stitches and variations that can be used to cover seams and embellish narrow fabric strips. Other types of embroidery, however, can be used to create a rich variety of design effects. These are among the few decorative elements you can preplan and complete before stitching the foundation.

Cross Stitch

A cross stitch piece is a good, easy way to incorporate your name and a date into the crazing quilting, as well as a pictorial design. You can create your own cross stitch motif or select one from a favorite cross stitch design book. A cross stitch piece can be an excellent center focus for a project made to honor a graduation, wedding or new baby, complete with name, dates and other statistics. Cross stitch fabrics come in a wide variety of weaves and colors.

Outline Embroidery

Victorian crazy quilts feature a multitude of outline embroideries. Animals, children and flowers were favorite motifs. Many of the Victorian embroidery patterns are still available today, as are more modern design books.

The outline stitch is also called the stem stitch. When used properly, it makes a fine line (see Stitch Dictionary, Page 74).

Use tissue paper and a transfer pencil to transfer the design onto your fabric, and your design books will remain intact. If your fabric is light enough, you might be able to see the design through the fabric to trace (a sunny window is a great help in this, for those who do not own a lightbox). Some favorite motifs are outline drawings of hands or baby feet. Duplicate a child's drawing for a juvenile project, or borrow ideas from a coloring book. A special pet or place can be highlighted in the work.

Outline embroidery is the most frequently used technique to create pictorial scenes in crazy quilting.

Examples of Outline Embroidery from Victorian crazy quilts

Crewel Embroidery

Crewel work is embroidery worked with wool on any kind of fabric. It derives its name from a firm, two-ply needlework wool also known as crewel.

This type of embroidery tends to favor flowers and animals. It is always worked with a large-eyed, blunt needle on fabric stretched tightly in an embroidery hoop. Some of the stitches offered in the Stitch Dictionary can be used for filler stitches in crewel.

Crewel is not as fine and delicate as outline embroidery, because it is worked with wool. Appropriate designs for crewel are usually less detailed than those used for outline.

Punchneedle Embroidery

Punchneedle embroidery is an old Russian technique that uses a special tiny needle threaded with embroidery floss or silk. The fabric is stretched, drum tight, in an embroidery hoop and the design is worked from the back. The result is a carpet of tiny loops that create the design on the right side with the look of thick plush. The loops can be sheared to give the design a velvety look. The work is very durable and washable.

Punchneedle embroidery can be used to highlight a pattern in a special fabric. If the design of the fabric shows through to the back, you can follow the lines to punchneedle parts of the pattern.

The beauty of this technique is that it's very fast and pretty. Any embroidery pattern can be used, even line drawings from coloring books and magazines.

There are several types and sizes of needles suitable for punchneedle, that will hold single strands, three strands or six strands of floss. Metallic threads can be used to good effect with this technique. To learn more about this type of embroidery, I recommend the book by Miranda Brown-Stewart, Ideas and Inspirations, A Punchneedle Techniques Primer. (See Source List, Page 80, for further information on these products.)

This is the 1930's crazy quilt made by the author's grandmother, Bessie Burns Baker. At right is a closeup look at a World War I souvenir handkerchief from the quilt. At the far right is a photo of Mrs. Baker with the author's father as a baby. He remembers his mother working on this quilt by lamplight. It incorporates fabrics from family clothings, as well as other personal mementos. 76" × 64". Courtesy of Mr. & Mrs. S. Lange.

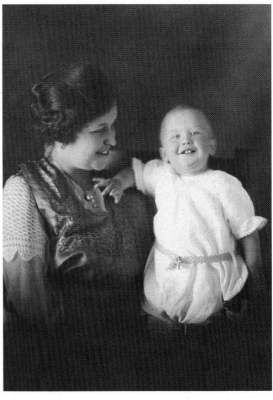

23A. (Above) This banner-like quilt was made in 1884 by Jesse Edgar. Made of silk brocades and velvets, it is highly embroidered with initials and outlines of children and flowers. The borders are 5" wide red velvet. American, 77" × 45".

23B. (Above, right) This is an unusual crazy quilt, made in the late 1800's. There are four fans per square, made of narrow strips of multi-colored satins and brocades. Black velvet corners come together to form center motifs, which are embellishments with purchased appliques. 64" × 66".

23C. (Right) This quilt is a small lace-edged sofa throw, made in the early 1890's by Mrs. William N. Byers for her infant son, Alfred, who later died at a very young age. The butterfly and embroidered name, shown in detail below, are worked with metallic threads. American, 32" × 66".

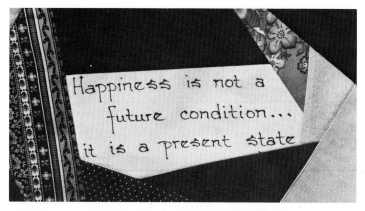

CALLIGRAPHY

Those blessed with fine penmanship, or who have taken a course in calligraphy, can add poetry, quotations and/or signatures to their crazy quilting. Use a fine-line pen that is permanent and washable. It's not a bad idea to test the pen on scrap fabric first. Even the most unartistic can use this type of pen to trace line drawings that can be included in the piecework.

FABRIC PAINTING

The Victorians used oils to paint pictures on fabric. This must have taken some time, as oils dry very slowly, but it certainly was faster than making embroidered pictures.

Today, we have acrylic paints that are more suitable to fabric painting. They can be used right out of the tube for a painterly look, or watered down and used like water color. These paints dry very quickly and can be painted over in a matter of minutes. Be sure the paint doesn't dry on the brush, or it won't come out and the brush will be ruined. Set the painting by pressing it, from the back, into a towel for wall hangings and pictures that won't be handled. If the piece will be actively used, then set it by soaking a cloth in vinegar and using it as a pressing cloth over the painting.

Some fabric dyes are suitable for painting and they lend a wonderful quality to the work. Check at your local craft shop for these products. They generally require that the fabric first be treated with an extender, then the dye is applied with a paint brush. When the picture is complete, the dye must be heat set. Use a pressing cloth over the picture and an iron set at medium heat.

Top: Use a fine, permanent marker to add calligraphy to your work.

Left and above: The owls and rose are examples of Victorian oil painting. The reptile is a contemporary work by Alice Bertling, highlighted with punchneedle embroidery.

FABRIC DYES

Fabric dying gives you more control over the colors of your project, particularly if you want a wide range of shadings. The dye is diluted with water, yet the colors can still be bright and wonderful. Dye, however, marks everything it touches, so it is best to work in a controlled environment. This is *not* a project for the kitchen counter with small children and pets underfoot. Keep a bucket of water nearby to deal with spills, and work with a sheet of plastic over your worktable or you'll risk ruining it.

If you want to try fabric dying, see if your local craft or fabric store offers a class. There are variations to this process, in which the dye is applied to wet fabric. The intensity of the color usually pales as the fabric dries. It is best to work with fabric pieces no larger than one yard.

MARBLIZING

Marblized fabric is something like moire, but with more colors. The process uses acrylic paint and carrageen, a suspension medium, mixed so that the paint floats on the surface of the water. Marblizing paper is a favorite for Girl Scouts and is done pretty much the same way as described here.

First, the fabric must be treated with a solution of alum and water. You should be able to get aluminum ammonium sulfate at your local drugstore. Dissolve 2 tbs. alum in 1 pint of hot water, and let the solution cool to room temperature before using it. Brush one side of the fabric with the alum water. This is the side that will be printed, so mark it with a small X. Allow the alum solution to saturate the fabric for at least 20 minutes before beginning, or wait for the fabric to dry.

Meanwhile, gather the equipment you'll need for painting. You need paper or plastic cups for the paint, toothpicks for placing paint on water, and narrow strips of newspaper for removing old paint from the water surface. Aluminum roasting pans make good marblizing trays. Lastly, you need a comb that is as wide as the marblizing pan. You might be able to buy one wide enough, or you can make out out of plastic curler pins. For fine lines of color, space the teeth ¼″ apart and tape them onto two pieces of wood or cardboard. For wider lines, space the teeth ½″ apart.

In the blender, add 1 tsp. of carrageen to one quart of moving (important) water. Blend about one minute until carrageen is completely dissolved. Pour this solution into the marblizing pan. Next, mix the acrylic paint with *distilled water,* until it is the consistency of thin cream. Use a separate cup for each paint color.

Dip a toothpick into the paint, then lightly touch the paint to the surface of the water. Work with as many colors as you like, using the comb to swirl the paint around, making streams of paint floating on the water.

Gently lay the fabric down on the water, just for a few seconds. Lift the fabric and rinse the printed side with clear water. Lay the fabric on towels to dry. You should be able to get two prints before having to remove the old paint and begin again. To pick up the paint, just skim the newspaper strips over the water. When the water is clean, begin again, creating new patterns with the

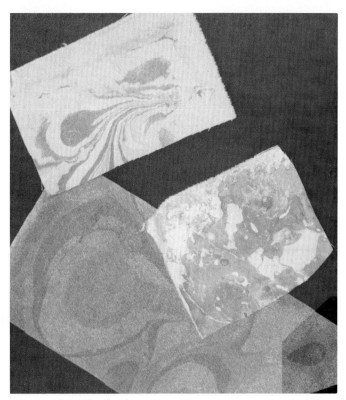

Samples of Marblized Fabric

paint, so that each marblized fabric piece is unique. When the fabric is completely dry, press carefully it with a warm iron.

PHOTOGRAPHY ON FABRIC

Black and white photographs, old and new, can be transferred to fabric with a special process called sun printing. Use family pictures or antique photos and the results will be great. The Source List (Page 80) includes a listing for sun printing materials that enable you to try this process at home. Briefly, it requires that the fabric be treated with a chemical solution, after which it is sandwiched, with the negative, between cardboard and glass, then exposed to the sun.

Example of a sun print on muslin, using an antique photo

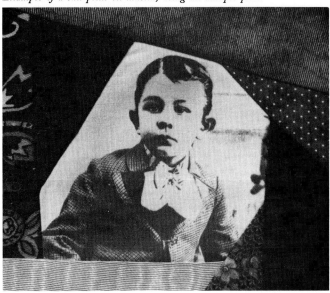

Ribbons make fun, colorful embellishments on crazy quilt projects. On their own, or used with other embellishments, ribbons can cover seams or create a dimensional effect. The photo above shows several ways to use ribbon. From upper left (clockwise), the techniques shown are rosettes (highlighted with French knots and Lazy Daisy), a twisted ribbon bow (tacked with French knots), meandering ribbon (tacked with beads), prairie points, a large rose with ribbon leaves, embroidered ribbon (with added button trim), wrapped ribbon roses with ribbon leaves, and a ruffled ribbon.

RIBBONS AND ROSES

The variety of ribbon offered today make crazy quilting more fun than ever. Most ribbon is polyester and will not fade or shrink.

Different widths of ribbon can be used in different ways. Wide ribbon can be sewn like a fabric piece right into the base work. Wide moire ribbon comes in a rainbow of colors, and wide woven ribbons can add quaint scenes to the pattern of the work.

Medium and narrow ribbons can be appliqued down to cover seam lines or to add interest to the fabric piece. These are a nice canvas on which to highlight special embroidery stitches. Very narrow ribbon can be woven through lace or twisted and tacked down with French knots.

Metallic and printed ribbons add to the effects of color, pattern and texture. They act as accents and do not need further embellishment. Grosgrain ribbon adds texture and is a pretty counterpoint to shiny satin. Don't overlook velvet ribbon, which is also polyester/nylon and will take a lot of use. Jacquard ribbon is available in an array of woven patterns and colors. Some of these are contoured with metallic threads.

Ribbon Seam Covers

Lay a ribbon directly over the seam line and applique it down on both sides. On most ribbons, it is nice to decorate them with embroidery stitches. Feather stitch is very effective, as are French knots, beads and Lazy Daisies. Use embroidery floss that contrasts nicely with the ribbon.

Meandering Ribbons

Japanese silk ribbon can be used to decorate a fabric piece or wander over several. This ribbon is usually ¼" wide and is very soft and pliable; it handles almost like bias. It is available in a wide range of colors, too. Use this ribbon to create interesting patterns over the base work. The ribbon can be tacked in place with beads or French knots, spaced close together to prevent the ribbon from snagging.

Ribbon Ruffles

Wide ribbons (1½" and wider) make nice little ruffles. Just run a gathering stitch down the center of the ribbon and pull the thread to gather. For a full ruffle, use double the length of ribbon. Even out the gathers and sew the ruffle to the base by hand or by machine. Ruffles can be highlighted with French knots or beads.

Twisted Ribbon & Bows

Twisted ribbon designs are pretty as fillers for fabric pieces. The ribbon can be tacked in place with beads or French knots. Choose a design — a bow, a snake-like zigzag or a heart, for example. Cut the ribbon 1¾ times the length needed. Anchor one end of the ribbon in place with a bead or French knot. If you're trying to form a specific shape, lightly trace the shape onto the fabric, then follow the lines with the ribbon, twisting it as you go. Place a knot or bead to secure each twist, then work back and place one at intermediate points. If the beads or knots are too far apart, the ribbon will snag.

Ribbon Prairie Points

Prairie points can be made with materials other than ribbon. They can be sewn directly into a seam or tucked under a lace edging, and decorated with beads or French knots. Use a ribbon at least 1″ wide, cut twice the width to form a rectangle (A). Fold down the top corners to the center of the bottom edge to form a triangle (B). Press the triangle shape flat (C). The ribbon prairie point can be used on either side.

Wrapped Ribbon Roses

These roses are gathered and wrapped for a soft, pretty look, whether large or small.

To make an average size rose, use a ribbon ¾″ wide, cut 3″ long. Lay it down flat and turn the ends down at right angles, then run a gathering stitch along the bottom edge (A). Pull the thread to gather; at the same time begin to wrap the ribbon around and around. Stitch the bottom of the rose tightly, then cut off the dangling ribbon ends. Sew the rose in place.

Wrapped roses can also be made with lace or narrow strips of folded fabric.

Large Ribbon Roses

These roses are big and wonderful. They are folded free-form so that each is unique, therefore more like real roses. For a large rose, use ribbon 1¼″ or wider, cut 5″ long. Make a slightly smaller rose with ribbon ¾″ wide, cut 4″ long.

Sew the ends of the ribbon together to make a circle (A). Gather with a running stitch close to one edge. Pull the circle closed, keeping the gathers even (B). Fold the circle into a rose shape (C) and stitch the bottom of the ribbon tightly to hold the shape. Sew the rose in place on the base.

Ribbon Rosettes

Small rosettes add a very delicate look to your work. Use narrow ribbon (¼″ to ¾″ wide), cut about 3″ long. Fold under one end and baste along one long edge (A). Gather tightly. Overlap the folded edge over the raw edge and stitch (B). If you use thread that matches the ribbon, you can use it to sew the rosette directly onto the fabric. Tack it only where the edges meet.

Ribbon Prairie Points

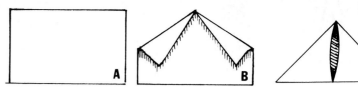

Wrapped Ribbon Roses

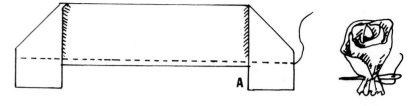

Large Ribbon Roses

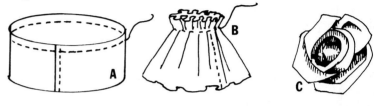

Ribbon Rosettes

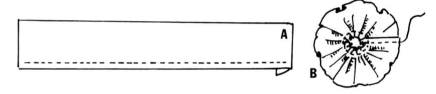

Ribbon Leaves

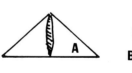

These flowers are very effective in a group. Add lazy daisy leaves and fill in the centers with French knots or beads.

Ribbon Leaves

To complement your ribbon or fabric roses, make leaves of ribbon, too. Cut a 1″ wide ribbon 1½″ long and fold it like a prairie point (A). Gather the wide edge with a basting stitch (B), then tack the leaf in place under the rose.

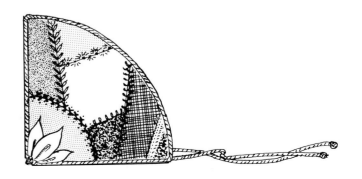

Example of 1920's beading

BEADS

Beads were seldom used on antique quilts made in America, but they were quite popular in England. The English favored smaller crazy quilt items such as pillows, foot stools and tea cozies, and many of these were richly beaded. In contemporary work, beads can be used in place of French knots or on their own to highlight a pattern or an embroidery. They add another element of texture to the work.

Good beads come in a wide variety of shapes, sizes, colors and finish. Each contributes a different effect to a crazy quilt project. Opaque seed beads come in solid colors. A cut glass bead reflects light like crystal — these are beautiful, but relatively expensive. Transparent beads glitter and sparkle. The luster seed bead had a metallic look, while the iris bead had a deep, iridescent lustre. The best quality beads are often imported from Italy or Czechoslovakia.

A well-stocked craft shop will have beads in a range of sizes, usually 10 to 13. The projects in this book feature size 11 beads, considered an average size.

Needles & Thread

The best results in beading require a few specialty items. When sewing with beads, always use a proper beading needle and nymo thread.

Beading needles come in a range of sizes and lengths. A long, thin needle, called a beading needle, is used only when putting on rows of beads, when the needle must be long enough to pick up perhaps 20 beads at a time. A shorter needle, called a sharp, is best for crazy quilting because you are usually sewing beads on one at a time. This needle is stronger than a beading needle and is long enough for short rows of beads.

The proper size of the needle depends on the size of the bead. The rule of thumb is to use the next highest number for the needle. For example, if you are working with #12 beads, you'll want a #13 needle.

Use nymo thread for all bead work. It is made just for beading and nothing else is as good. It looks like dental floss and is available at some craft shops. If you have a problem finding nymo thread, refer to the Source List, Page 80.

Many beaded garments made in the 1920's and 30's are literally coming apart because the beading thread is disintegrating. Regular thread gives way over time and the beads will be lost. Nylon filament will stretch and is very stiff. With nymo thread, our bead work will be in good shape five years or 50 years from now.

Embroidery Highlights

When beads are used to accent embroidery, they are sewn on one at a time. Pour out a few beads at a time into a shallow dish so they can be picked up easily with the needle. Do not try to work with them from the storage container, as this can be very awkward and frustrating.

Bring the needle up at the point of the stitch, pick up a bead on the needle, then go back down into the fabric through the same hole. Pull the thread with a bounce to lodge the bead securely into the fabric. Go on to the next stitch and do the same.

As a precaution, I like to tie a knot at the back of every fourth bead. This way, if a bead is pulled off, it won't start a chain reaction and the other beads will stay in place.

Use beads to highlight stitches such as the feather stitch, cretan, herringbone and the buttonhole. Use it in place of a French knot for a varied effect.

Sewn Beadwork

To make flower stems or leaf veins with beads, the beads are sewn on in rows. Beaded lines can curve, too, so they make excellent flowers and other shapes.

On a long, narrow beading needle, pick up as many beads as are needed for the line. Let them fall down the thread and into position on the fabric. Put the needle down through the fabric and pull gently. Now come up at every third bead and couch between the beads, pulling the thread tightly. This is called the Lazy Squaw stitch — perhaps the more industrious squaws couched down every bead!

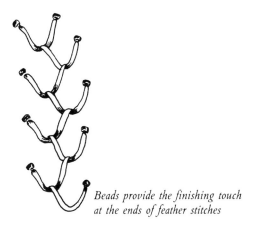

Beads provide the finishing touch at the ends of feather stitches

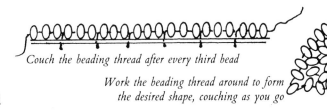

Couch the beading thread after every third bead

Work the beading thread around to form the desired shape, couching as you go

Example of American Indian beadwork

KNOTS & OTHER THINGS

Sometimes, the right finishing touch elevates a nice project to a terrific one. That extra detail of something special can make a dramatic difference. For extra pizzazz, you might consider making knots and loops, instead of an ordinary button closure on garments, or to add texture to other projects. Cording finishes a garment like nothing else. And tassels are fun decorations for garments, quilts, pillows and other projects.

Chinese Button Balls

Loops and button balls, made of rat-tail cording, add a rich look of detail to crazy quilt garments. Button balls take a little practice to make well, but the effect is worth the effort. Use about 6″ of cording for each ball. Follow the illustration below to make as many knotted balls as desired, leaving at least a 1″ tail to sew into the seam.

Chinese Button Balls

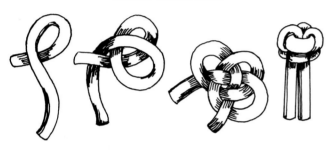

Knotted Loops

Loops make nice closures on many garments, with a knot or a button. Or, you might just like loops for their own sake for the texture they create.

A 6″ length of rat-tail cord makes a good size loop. Fold the cord in half (1) and tie a loose slip knot close to the open end (2), as illustrated below. Manipulate the knot with your fingers to flatten it (3).

Knotted Loops

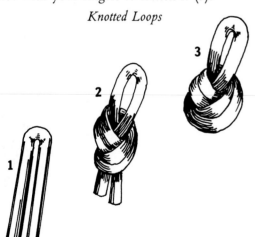

On most garments, loops and balls are sewn into a seam, but on some projects, like the crazy quilt evening bag, this is impossible. When this is the case, tuck the loose ends of the cording under and tack the knot in place, using strong thread that is the same color as the cording.

Tassels

The Victorians loved tassels and used them generously on quilts and pillow corners. Tassels are great to hang off wall hangings or to decorate closures on garments. They are easy to make, in any size you like, but expensive to buy.

I recommend making tassels with silk buttonhole twist. Use a piece of cardboard as wide as you want your tassel to be long; for example, use a 3″ wide cardboard for a 3″ long tassel. Wind the thread around the cardboard (1). The more thread you use, the fatter the tassel. Gather the thread at the top and tie (2) using a thread long enough that it will serve later to attach the tassel to the project. Clip the other end of the tassel and remove the cardboard. Now, wind a neck around the tied end (3), using matching thread. If necessary, tie a thread onto the end for attaching the tassel to the finished item.

Tassels

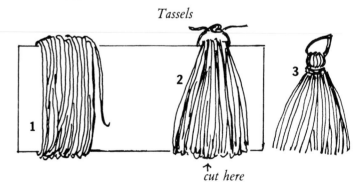

cut here

Cording

Cording is very important to give a professional finished look to a crazy quilted garment. It is not difficult to make or apply; most general sewing texts give step-by-step instructions. Covered cording ties make a nice front closure on some garments, too.

BUTTONS

Buttons are a quick, easy source of color, shape and texture. They can be ceramic, shell, mother of pearl, bone, leather, metal or plastic, or covered with complimentary fabric. Buttons can add a touch of whimsy to crazy quilting. They can march along in neat rows or bunch up in interesting clusters. Buttons can accent a ribbon, or hold a bow in place. It's fun to use a lot of buttons in crazy quilting, so keep a big supply on hand.

Look for buttons in antique shops, garage sales and estate sales, as well as traditional fabric shops. At many stores, your best buy will be discontinued packets sold at a discount. But I don't mind spending more for antique buttons if they are just the right touch to finish off a project. One of my favorite antique shops saves all its Victorian jet buttons for me, because they know I'm a sure sale. Antique pearl buttons are such a pretty touch for crazy quilting and they are not difficult to find. Reproductions of old pearl buttons are available at many fabric stores.

Used in rows, tiny pearl baby buttons are especially effective. They almost look like flowers if you sew them on with yellow silk thread and edge them with green Lazy Daisy stitches.

Make interesting shapes with buttons. To make a paisley shape, start out with a large, flat button and rotate outward, decreasing the button size, to achieve the desired shape. Ball buttons make nice clusters, especially in a mix of sizes and colors.

Sew buttons onto the basework with silk buttonhole twist, using a complimentary color. This forms visual interest. Sometimes, you can add beads to the buttonholes as you sew.

Treat the use of buttons like lace. If the buttons are very old and valuable, put them on projects that will get little handling. Use them in special gift pictures and wall hangings. It's hard to resist adding them onto a special garment, though. If an antique button will finish off a clothing project, then use it but make sure it's sewn on securely and tie double knots on the back. If a project is washable, use buttons that can stand up to repeated cleaning and use.

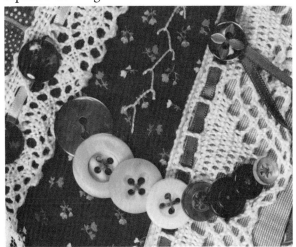

31A. (Top) Specialty buttons add a lot of fun to a crazy quilt scene, with little time and trouble. This simple scene is transferred by buttons in the shapes of sheep, cows, birds, cactus and moon. See Source List, Page 80.

31B. (Above) Clusters of buttons are more fun than just one! These show how they can be used to hold ribbon bows in place, and how they can be sewn on with beads.

31C. (Left) Making shapes with groups of buttons, like this snail shape, is another way of creating interesting visual effects with buttons.

LACES, DOILIES & HANKIES

Lace acts as an element of texture in crazy quilting. By laying lace or a doily over a deep, rich color, you add an element of drama. Laces, old and new, can decorate seams or accent a dull fabric.

Use long, narrow pieces of lace to overlay the seams of the crazy quilting. These can be tacked down on both sides with an applique stitch or machine sewn with matching thread. They can be highlighted with ribbon or embroidery stitches. (Lace or doilies can be tacked down with embroidery stitches, too.) Add beads for sparkle, or small buttons. Colored lace can carry through a color scheme. White or off-white lace, applied to a pastel fabric, takes on a muted, softer look. Keep lace embellishments in the same mood as the rest of the work.

Ruffled lace adds a soft, feminine look to crazy quilt projects. A good example is the Victorian Christmas stocking shown on Page 59.

When using lace, keep in mind how much wear and the kind of use a finished project will receive. This may help you decide whether to use that special heirloom lace. The price and/or sentimental value will determine if you can cut into it. Most new laces are either cotton or polyester, so they can be washed. You can minimize the starkness of new lace by tea dying.

An old lacy handkerchief, embroidered and embellished with buttons, is preserved forever in the friendship quilt pictured on the back cover. Laces, doilies and hankies can be used this way, to cover seams, or to be a special focus of attention in crazy quilting.

Cleaning Antique Lace

Old lace, doilies and hankies are found at antique and secondhand shops, estate sales and garage sales. However, many lovely old pieces are soiled and stained and must be cleaned carefully before they can be used.

Try washing stained lace by hand in a mild detergent. Wrap it in a towel and squeeze out excess water, then let the lace dry flat. If stains persist, use a mixture of lemon with mild detergent, then let the lace dry on green grass. Then, rinse thoroughly and dry again. The chlorophyll in the grass helps bleach out the stain. Diluted laundry bleach might work on tough stains, but it must be rinsed very thoroughly and the lace washed after bleaching.

If all efforts to clean a stain fail, try cutting away the stained parts, or just accept the stain as part of the antiquity of the piece. Or, let the stain dictate the look and tea dye the entire piece to match.

Tea Dying

Light colored laces and fabrics, steeped in tea, take on a patina of age that is charming. The slightly yellowed effect can effectively camouflage some stains. Best of all, tea dying is as easy as brewing a cup of tea.

To make the tea solution, boil a gallon of water with four tea bags in it for 15 minutes. Strain the solution and return it to simmer. Wet the lace in plain water, then put it into the simmering tea. When the lace has simmered for 15 minutes, take it out and put it in a setting solution of ½ cup white vinegar in one gallon of water. Let it set for 15 minutes, then rinse it thoroughly and press.

If the stain is still obvious, repeat the dying process, letting the lace simmer longer.

Doilies

Small doilies can be used whole or cut into fan shapes for spectacular effects. Many of today's machine-made doilies are good reproductions of old patterns. These pieces — round, oval, rectangle or square — add a wonderful element of shape, texture and color to the work. A doily covers a multitude of sins if the your seams aren't quite perfect. Be sure a doily is tacked down in several places to prevent it from snagging.

Hankies

Handkerchiefs, especially old ones, can be a wonderful design source. Many old hankies have beautiful tatted and crocheted edges, or fancy embroidered initials. Many have wonderful corners that make great triangular pieces for the basework. Hankies generally add a soft, feminine touch as well as a feeling of old fashioned elegance.

PROJECTS

Now it's time to put our theories into practice. The following pages feature fullsize patterns and step-by-step directions for 10 crazy quilt projects. Use these projects to gain experience with crazy quilt techniques and confidence in your design ability. Then branch out to design projects of your own — Christmas decorations, tablecloths, full size quilts, etc.

Yardages given are based on 44/45" wide fabrics.

Plastic "Window" Templates

You may have seen an artist squint through a small circle he's made with his hands. By doing this, he eliminates all the surrounding distractions to concentrate on his subject.

Quilters can do something similar with window templates. Using opaque plastic (generally available at quilt shops), cut out a window the exact size and shape of the finished project. This window lets you see only the design area, eliminating the distraction of unfinished edges, seam allowances, etc.

The crazy quilt foundation is always cut larger than the pattern outline. While this allows for shrinkage, it also gives you room to play with design placement. By moving the window around on the foundation, twisting and angling it, you can choose just the right combination of color and shape.

I use the window templates for all my jewelry, small pictures and needlecases. Try this device when you next work on a small project; you'll find it can open doors to better design.

FANCY CRAZY QUILT
WALL HANGING

This wall hanging is a good starter piece. It is a small project but it incorporates many lessons and challenges of crazy quilting. Victorian fans, used in each corner, give a nice feeling of balance and symmetry. These are pieced and added after the base crazy quilting is done. The center medallion shown is a piece of contemporary crazy quilting, a scene. The medallion can also be used to highlight a special piece of embroidery or memento. To make this project even easier, you can omit the medallion and make an overall design. Work with a color scheme in mind. You can use fancy fabrics, like the wall hanging pictured on Page 33, or create a completely different look with "homey" fabrics such as wool, cotton and suede cloth.

Finished size 30″ × 40″

Materials Needed:
Fabrics —
   Scraps of at least 12 different fabrics for
      basework (silks, velvet, moire, chintz, etc.)
   1 yard pre-washed muslin for basework
   1 yard pretty fabric for backing
      (add ¼ yard for a hanging sleeve)
   ½ yard for borders (satin, velvet or moire)
   ⅓ yard for binding

Other Materials —
   Embroidery floss or silk buttonhole twist
   Beads, beading needle and nymo thread
   Assorted lace, ribbon and button trim
   Metallic threads, if desired
   24″ of string and a pencil

1. Cut or tear the prewashed muslin to 24″ × 34″. This will be the base piece and it allows for 2″ of extra fabric all around.

2. Tie one end of the string to the pencil to serve as a make-shift compass. Mark the string 9″ from the pencil and again at 17″ from the pencil. (Illustration #1)

17″   9″

Illustration #1

3. Grasp the string at the 9″ mark and hold it at one corner of the muslin. Swing the pencil out and mark an arc on the muslin. Repeat at each corner to outline the positions of the fans. Now position the 17″ mark at each corner to make large swinging lines as shown in Illustration #2. These outline the center medallion.

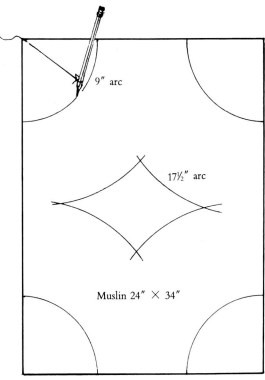

Illustration #2

4. Make the center medallion separate from the base piece. Copy the shape onto another piece of muslin, adding ½″ for seam allowances all around. Fill in the medallion with a scene as shown or another motif of your choice. The medallion is a great way to highlight a picture, a signature or anything special that you want to be the main focus of the wall hanging.

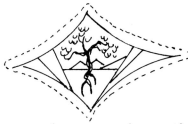

5. Make four corner fans, separate from the muslin base, in the same way. (Fan pattern is on Page 38.) Each fan has four segments. Press under a ¼″ seam allowance on the curved edge of each completed fan.

6. Cut borders before beginning to sew. For square corners, cut two side borders each 4¼″ × 22½″ and two borders 4¼″ × 41″. For mitered corners, cut two border strips 4¼″ × 31″ and two strips 4¼″ × 41″. Cut up any remaining border fabric to use in the basework.

Instructions continue on Page 38

36A. This crazy quilt was made in 1920 by the members of the Plymouth Daughters, a women's group of the Congregational Church of Arkansas City, Kansas. Made of wool and linen, it was a farewell gift to the wife of the church pastor, Mrs. George T. Nichols, who carried it to her new home in Denver, Colorado. The names on the patches are seventeenth century names taken from Calvinist virtues of the time. Each member of the Plymouth Daughters assumed one of the names. Other names that appear are of church-goers who contributed to making the gift. 86" × 140".

36C. & 36D. Crazy quilting is for everyone, including children. At top, Joy Carlsen models a green cotton dress with crazy quilt shoulders and antique handkerchief bodice. The pattern is a simple T-dress made sleeveless for summer sun. Below, Tracy Carlsen's sundress is decorated with a crazy quilt fan. Embroidery and colorful ribbon complete the look. Andy Simpson's vest is made from a commercial pattern, decorated with a crazy quilt farm scene. Special animal buttons make extra fun. Cotton fabrics make the garments easy to wear and wash.

36B. This quilt is notable for the many hand painted pieces by the quiltmaker, Augusta Ernestine Houck. Made in 1894, the quilt includes some fabrics from the gowns of several Colorado governors, as well as campaign ribbons and special event ribbons. 60" × 60".

37A. (Right) This quilt, made circa 1884, has outstanding examples of applique and embroidery. Peacock, calla lily, Greenaway children, cat and butterfly embroideries are among the embroidered designs; appliques include an umbrella and a paint palette. Although the maker's name is unknown, the initials L.V. are embroidered near the bottom of the quilt. American, 56" × 60".

37B. Madeleine Montano models a dress embellished with crazy quilting, which shows that pastels can be used with great success. The dress is made with shoulder pieces that come over the bodice almost to the waistline. Streamers of ribbon complete the look, reminiscent of an old-fashioned English garden.

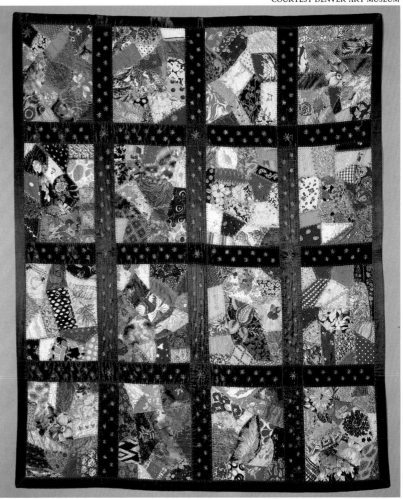

37C. (Right) This is a wonderful quilt from 1940, showcasing silks and mixed fabrics. Made by Eva M. Swanson (1882-1980), the quilt is made of 16 rectangles, each with 4" wide borders. The border strips are decorated with Lazy Daisy embroidery in various colors. 86" × 70".

7. Now fill in the base piece with random crazy quilting. Let the edges of the fabric pieces slightly overlap the areas outlined for the medallion and fans; these will be covered later when the separate pieces are appliqued in place. (Illustration #4)

Illustration #4

8. Turn under the seam allowances of the medallion and press them flat. Position the medallion carefully over the basework and pin it in place. With a blind stitch, applique the medallion onto the base. Then, do the same for each of the corner fans.

9. Press the whole piece, making sure everything lies nice and flat. Carefully measure and cut the base piece down to 22½″ × 32½″.

10. The wall hanging is now ready for the decorative details. Add lace and ribbon, blindstitching them down securely. Cover the seams with Victorian stitches (see Stitch Dictionary, Page 65). Highlight stitches with beads as desired. Add embroidered fans and spider webs on plan fabrics. Sew on buttons last.

11. Sew on borders, using a ¼″ seam allowance. Sew side borders on first, then top and bottom. Corners can be square or mitered. Trim excess fabric at corners.

12. Cut the backing fabric to 30″ × 40″ and pin it to the quilt. Tack backing to front by taking small hidden stitches from the front. (You can hide these under lace and embroidery stitches.) You might sew on a last button or two, sewing through all layers.

13. Cut the binding fabric into four strips, 3″ wide and the same length as the borders. Fold each strip in half lengthwise, so it is 1½″ wide, right sides out. With the raw edges neatly together, press the fold along the length of the strip.

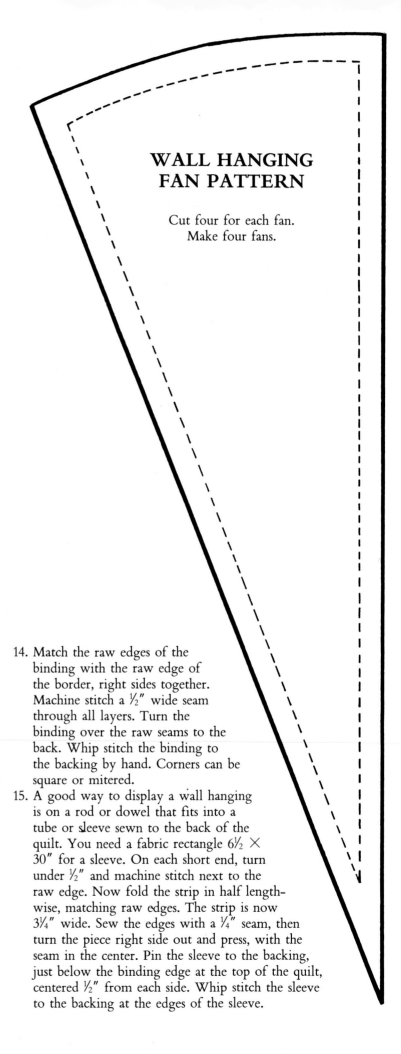

WALL HANGING FAN PATTERN

Cut four for each fan.
Make four fans.

14. Match the raw edges of the binding with the raw edge of the border, right sides together. Machine stitch a ½″ wide seam through all layers. Turn the binding over the raw seams to the back. Whip stitch the binding to the backing by hand. Corners can be square or mitered.

15. A good way to display a wall hanging is on a rod or dowel that fits into a tube or sleeve sewn to the back of the quilt. You need a fabric rectangle 6½ × 30″ for a sleeve. On each short end, turn under ½″ and machine stitch next to the raw edge. Now fold the strip in half lengthwise, matching raw edges. The strip is now 3¼″ wide. Sew the edges with a ¼″ seam, then turn the piece right side out and press, with the seam in the center. Pin the sleeve to the backing, just below the binding edge at the top of the quilt, centered ½″ from each side. Whip stitch the sleeve to the backing at the edges of the sleeve.

NEEDLECASE

A fast, lovely little project, a needlecase is very useful for anyone who sews. It is large enough to hold embroidery scissors, thread, needles and a thimble. With a hanging cord, it can be worn around your neck so your sewing needs are never lost or out of reach. Without the cord, it can be used in a sewing basket or attached to a belt as a decorative pocket. This is a really nice item to make for gifts. (See photo, Page 48.)

Finished size 4″ × 4½″

Materials Needed

Fabrics —
   Small scraps of 6-8 fancy fabrics
   8″ square prewashed muslin
   4″ square of felt
   6″ × 18″ moire or velvet
      for lining and backing

Other Materials —
   7″ × 14″ fleece or needlepunch
   Embroidery floss or silk buttonhole
      twist in three colors
   Beads, beading needle, nymo thread
   4½″ grosgrain ribbon (¼″ wide)
   74″ rat-tail cord
   Snaps or Velcro circles for closure
   Plastic for window template

1. This piece is an exercise in the Center Piece Method described on Page 16. On the muslin square, place a small piece of dark fabric at the center. This piece should have at least five angles. Working clockwise, sew down each fabric piece in turn. Keep the pieces small and irregularly shaped.
2. When the square is filled with crazy quilting, use a plastic window template or some other device to find a 4½″ × 5″ design area that you like. Mark this rectangle on the fabric, then cut away the excess.
3. Cover each seam with embroidery stitches (see Stitch Dictionary, Page 65.) Add special embellishments, such as embroidered initials, a spider web, beads, or buttons. This is a great way to personalize gifts for any recipient. Usually, the first angular piece is a good place to add such a highlight.
4. Cut two 4½″ × 5″ rectangles from the fleece. Cut three rectangles from the lining/backing fabric. Cut the felt 1″ smaller all around, 2½″ × 3″, using pinking shears for a nice edge.
5. Glue or tack the felt piece to the right side of one lining rectangle. On the right side of another lining piece,

add the grosgrain ribbon. Position the ribbon 1¼″ from the top edge and stitch it down at the ends, center and 1″ on either side of center, as illustrated below. This will be your scissor holder.

6. Lay the lining piece down, ribbon side up. Put the finished front piece over it, matching right sides. Finally, lay a piece of fleece on top. Put one pin in each side to hold the layers together as you work.
7. Using a ¼″ seam allowance, machine stitch all around; leave a 2″ opening in the center of one end for turning.
8. Trim the fleece ⅛″ from the seam to reduce bulk. Turn right side out and close the opening by hand.
9. Repeat the process for the back of the needlecase, layering the remaining backing piece (right side up) with the lining (felt side down) and the remaining fleece. Press both finished sections.
10. Whip stitch the two sections together, up to the designated line 1½″ from the top edge.
11. Cut 14″ of rat-tail cord for the edging. Fold over a small loop at one end of the cord and hold it in place at the needlecase edge as illustrated at right. With contrasting floss or buttonhole twist, wrap the loop in place. Continue around the bottom, whipping the cord to the edge. Finish off with another loop opposite the first.
12. Use remaining rat-tail to make a neck cord. Sew on snaps or Velcro circles at center top.

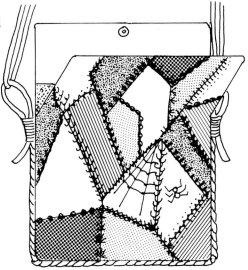

Tack ribbon in three places.

Stitch to this line on both sides

4″

Leave open for turning

40C. Fan Pendant. A simple pieced fan becomes sensational wearable art with the addition of embroidery, buttons and beads. See Page 46 for patterns and instructions.

40A. Desert Medallion. "Hot" and "cool" colors represent desert and distant mountains in this 4" round medallion. The flowering cactus is made of Chain, Lazy Daisy and French Knot stitches. A variety of stitches, complemented with beads, decorate seam lines. Patterns and instructions for this project are on Page 56.

40B. Evening Purses. The simple clutch purse is easy to make and fun to use. The crazy quilt back is offset by a solid bottom panel. Finished size is 4" × 8". Patterns and instructions are on Page 42.

41A. Heart Belt Buckles (above). A plain black silk sash belt achieves glamour status with the addition of a coordinated pair of crazy quilt hearts. Each heart is only 3½" wide. See Page 53 for instructions.

41B. Heart Bags (left). Small heart-shaped bags are great for both day and evening wear. Buttons, beads and embroidery enhance the individuality of each creation. Finished size is about 6" × 6". See Page 54 for project patterns and instructions.

41C. Heart Pendants (below). These are great as wearable art, but they're small enough (3½" wide) to be used as tree trimmers, door knob hangers, etc. Pattern and instructions for this versatile project are on Page 52.

EVENING ENVELOPE PURSE

Finished size 4″ × 8″

Materials needed:

Fabrics —
  Scraps of 10-12 assorted fancy fabrics
  Two pieces 9″ × 13″ prewashed muslin
  9″ × 13″ lining
  9″ × 5″ fabric for solid bottom section
  (can be same as lining)

Other Materials —
  9″ × 13″ fleece or needlepunch
  9″ × 13″ curtain buttress or buckram (seam
    two narrower pieces together, if necessary)
  Assorted lace, ribbon and button trim
  Beads, beading needle, nymo thread
  Embroidery floss or silk buttonhole twist
  46″ grosgrain ribbon (1″ wide) for binding*
  6″ rat-tail cord for loop
  1 fancy ball button for closure

  *You can use another material for binding, but
  grosgrain works best. It is usually heavier and
  sturdier than other ribbon; with use, silk or
  satin fibers will wear and give way.

1. The purse pattern is given in two halves on the
   opposite page. Trace the pattern onto one piece
   of muslin, joining the pattern sections to make a
   continuous shape 8½″ wide and 12½″ long. This
   includes a ¼″ seam allowance all around as indicated on the pattern. Use the tracing as a pattern
   to cut the same shape from the other muslin piece
   as well as the fleece, lining and buckram.

2. Mark the fold/seam lines on both muslin pieces
   and the lining.

3. Lay one muslin piece on a flat surface, marked
   side up. Position the fleece on top and pin it in
   place with just a few pins, strategically placed to
   keep the fleece from shifting as you work.

4. Starting at one corner of the top flap, begin random crazy quilting. Remove pins as you go so
   they won't interfere with the fabric laying flat.
   Work the crazy quilting down to ¼″ below the
   bottom seam/fold line.

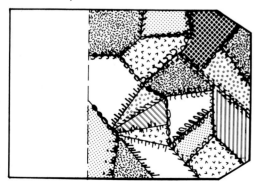

5. When the basework is done, sew on all desired lace and
   ribbons. Sew down all the edges so the trim won't snag
   when the purse is handled.

6. The 5″ × 9″ piece of outer fabric is slightly larger than
   needed. Center it on the basework, right sides together, so
   that one long edge is ¼″ below the
   seam/fold line. Machine stitch through all layers, sewing
   on the seam line. Press all fabrics flat, then trim the outer
   fabric even with the base.

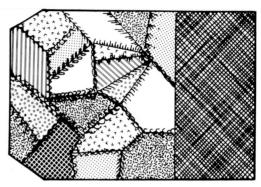

7. Now is the time for embroidery, beading, buttons and any
   other decorative details you wish to add.

8. Turn the finished crazy quilted piece face down. Lay the
   buckram on the back (muslin) side of the crazy quilting.
   Next, layer the second piece of muslin, then the lining
   (right side up). Pin layers together to hold.

9. Start sewing the binding at the top (solid piece) right corner. Working on the right side of the crazy quilting, machine stitch through all layers with a ¼″ seam. Stitch all
   the way around to the opposite corner, and trim ends
   even with the top edge.

10. Turn the binding over the seam allowance and whip stitch
    it onto the back.

11. Sew another piece of ribbon binding across the top straight
    edge of the purse. Turn it over and whip it in place on the
    back. Press binding flat.

12. Fold the purse in
    thirds on the mark-
    ed fold and seam
    lines. By hand, sew
    the sides of the pur-
    se together, just in-
    side the binding. Be
    sure to use strong
    thread and take
    small, tight stitches.

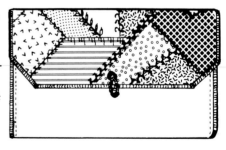

13. At the center of the angled flap, attach a knotted loop (see
    Decorative Details, Page 30). Fold the flap into its proper
    position on the purse and mark the place for the button,
    then sew it on.

PATTERN FOR EVENING PURSE

Join pattern pieces to make a single pattern 8½″ wide and 12½″ long

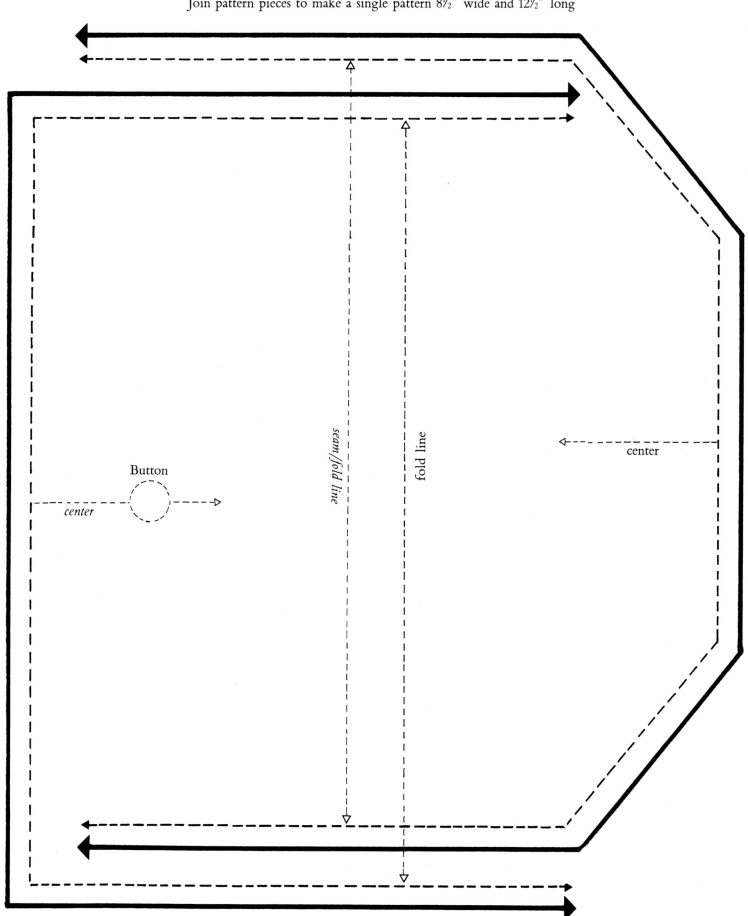

44A. This is a special T-dress the author made for her daughter's first Communion. The heart bodice is made of old family handkerchiefs and can be removed for framing or to make into a pillow when Madeleine outgrows the dress. The crazy quilting is done in soft pastels, complemented with ribbon, embroidery and button accents.

44B. This black wool cocktail dress is dramatized with an asymmetrical yoke and cuffs worked in crazy quilting. The crazy quilting, repeated in a back yoke, uses silk, satin and silk buttonhole twist.

44C. The author used a commercial pattern and drapery moire to create this lovely cocktail suit. The crazy quilt borders and cuffs are highlighted with punchneedle embroidery.

45A. Made from a polycotton fabric by Concord, this Indian-inspired garment is entitled "Arapaho West." The turquoise blouse, highlighted with crazy quilting, ribbons and punchneedle embroidery, is made from a Folkwear pattern (see Source List, Page 80).

45B. This crazy quilt vest has an overall design on the front and a V-yoke in back, made with silks and satins.

45C. Jason and Fred Montano show how crazy quilting can have a masculine look with the use of wool suiting, cotton shirting and denim. Heavy embroidery floss outlines every seam.

FAN NECKLACE

The fan necklace is very elegant. A large pendant, hung from a twisted multicolored cord, it incorporates the fan shape and Victorian stitches in an unusual way. The flower motif that highlights the top of the fan can be worked in needlepunch as shown in the photo on Page 40, or in other embroidery. If you prefer, substitute initials or a spider web. See Stitch Dictionary, Page 65.

Finished size 6½″ × 4¾″

Materials Needed
Fabrics —
    Scraps of six different fabrics for fan petals
    10″ square dark (black) cotton
      for embroidery motif
    Two 9″ squares of prewashed muslin
    9″ square of leather for backing*

Other Materials —
    9″ × 28″ fleece or needlepunch
    Embroidery floss or silk buttonhole twist
      (include 4 colors of floss for flower)
    Beads, beading needle and nymo thread
    9″ square of artboard
    Fabric glue
    Darning needle and strong thread
    Decorative buttons and/or other trim
    3 (different colors) 30″ lengths rat-tail cord
    20″ rat-tail cord for outer edging
    #3 size punchneedle for punchneedle
      embroidery (optional)

*Leather probably isn't an ordinary household item, nor is it inexpensive to buy. But I've tried every conceivable alternative and leather does work best. It is easily cleaned, it glues well, doesn't ravel and holds up to a lot of use. If you don't want to buy a piece of leather (many hobby shops sell small pieces), you can cut up an old purse that you don't use anymore.

1. If you're going to work an embroidery motif on the top fan piece, complete it first. Trace the outline of the fan top pattern onto the dark cotton fabric, then trace the embroidery design in the center of it. Work the motif in punchneedle or other embroidery stitches.

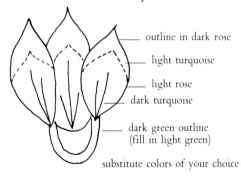

outline in dark rose
light turquoise
light rose
dark turquoise
dark green outline (fill in light green)
substitute colors of your choice

2. Cut out six fan petals, from six different fabrics. Decide how you want them positioned, from left to right.

3. Use one muslin square as a backing for the fan pieces. Sew the fan spokes together, stitching through both seam allowances and through the muslin square.

4. Applique the embroidered fan top onto the fan piece, overlapping the ends of the fan spokes. Press the fan flat, then trim away the excess muslin around the fan.

5. Add decorative details, including beads and buttons. Cover each seam with embroidery stitches.

6. Using the fan base pattern, cut out one fan shape of leather, one of cardboard, one from the remaining muslin square and three of fleece. Starting at the bottom, stack the fan pieces in the following order: muslin, artboard, three fleece and, finally, the finished crazy quilted fan. The crazy quilt fan piece will be quite a bit larger than the others.

7. With a darning needle and strong thread, whip stitch the fan to the bottom muslin piece, over the fleece and artboard. Stitch around twice; on the second round, dig deeper into the muslin to pull the assembly taut. The corners of the fan may have to be trimmed a bit for a good fit.

8. Tie the three 30″ neckcord pieces together with a knot at one end. Leave a ½″ tail below the knot. Twist the three cords together and make a similar knot at the other end.

9. Glue the leather onto the back of the assembled fan, using a generous amount of fabric glue. Hold the piece together tightly for a minute or two. It's okay to let a small amount of glue ooze out of the jointure.

10. While the glue is still wet, insert one tail of the neckcord between the leather backing and the muslin, using the dark flower piece as the insert point (see illustration below). Re-twist the cord and insert the other end.

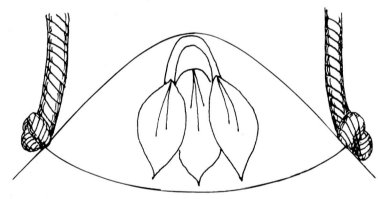

11. Glue the 20″ cord around the outer edge of the fan. When the glue is dry, whip stitch the cord in place.

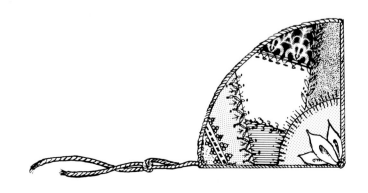

PATTERNS FOR FAN PENDANT

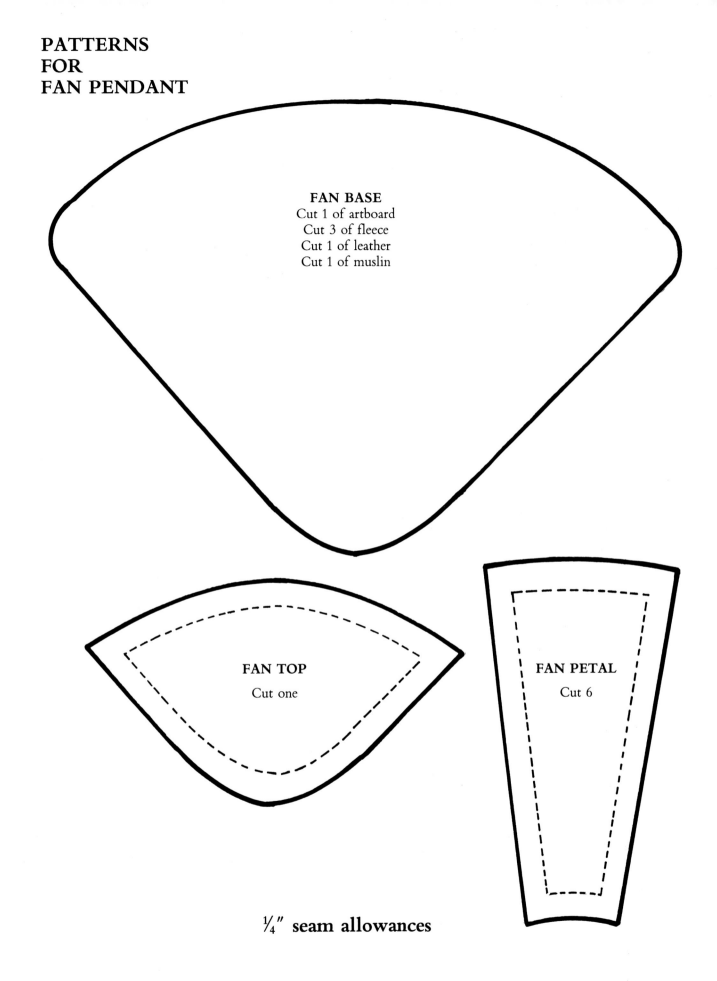

FAN BASE
Cut 1 of artboard
Cut 3 of fleece
Cut 1 of leather
Cut 1 of muslin

FAN TOP

Cut one

FAN PETAL

Cut 6

¼″ **seam allowances**

48A. Oval Belt Buckles (above). A simple black sash is a key to a versatile wardrobe when you add interchangeable oval motifs. Each oval is 3" × 4¼", and attaches to the belt with Velcro. Patterns and instructions begin on Page 60.

48B. Crazy Quilt Paintings (right). A 4" crazy quilt scene becomes a fabric painting, matted and framed. The frame is 8" square. Patterns and instructions for this project are on Page 49.

48C. Needlecases (below). A nice gift for sewing circle friends, this little needlecase holds needles, thread and embroidery scissors. Pattern and instructions are on Page 39.

CRAZY QUILT PAINTINGS

Crazy quilt paintings mix old with new, almost like painting with fabric to create a mood or a scene. With just the change of color or texture, each painting takes on a new and different look. These crazy quilt paintings are done with pattern pieces laid down string quilting style. They are then embellished with Victorian stitches and beads. It is usually best to keep to a two-color scheme (such as teal and rose, peach and blue). Use shades of the two colors, mixing in a variety of texture and pattern. Refer to the color photo on the facing page.

Finished size: 8″ square (framed)

Materials Needed

Fabrics —
    Small scraps appropriate for each scene, including sky blue
    8″ square prewashed muslin

Other Materials —
    6″ square fleece or needlepunch
    Embroidery floss or silk buttonhold twist
    8″ square cardboard or artboard
    Beads, beading needle and nymo thread
    White marking pencil or water erasable pen
    Glue
    Masking tape
    6″ square template plastic for window plus additional plastic for pattern templates
    8″ square mat board with 4″ circle cut out*
    8″ square frame*

*Many stores sell precut mats and easy-to-assemble frames. If you can't find what you want, go to a regular frame store, but be prepared to pay a higher price for custom-made items. For a more economical way, look in your Yellow Pages for a "do-it-yourself" frame shop. In this kind of store, you select materials that are cut for you, and the shop staff will help you to assemble the frame yourself.

1. Use the pattern on Page 57 to make a plastic window template.

2. Trace your choice of pattern in the center of the 8″ muslin square. Then, mark a second, outer circle, ½″ larger all around.

3. You can make any scene by cutting fabric pieces by hand as you go, or you can make a template for the pattern pieces given on Pages 50 and 51. The patterns given include seam allowances as indicated — ¼″ on inside seams and ½″ on the outside edges.

4. Sew the pieces down in numerical order, sewing on the marked lines. Press each piece flat before adding the next. If pattern lines are covered by another fabric, mark guidelines on the top fabric.

5. When all pieces are sewn and pressed, lay the window template over the piece. Mark the 4″ circle with white pencil or water erasable pen.

6. Sketch in a free-form tree, using water erasable pen. (Just a splash of cold water later will remove any tell-tale marks.) Use embroidery floss or silk buttonhole twist to make a tree trunk of Stem Stitches. Use the Feather Stitch to make twigs and leaves. (See Stitch Dictionary, Page 65.)

7. Cover the seams with embroidery stitches. Add beads to highlight the stitches.

8. Center the finished picture in the mat opening. Pull the fabric tight behind the circle opening. Tape it in place from the back with masking tape.

9. Cut out a 4″ circle of fleece. With the picture laying face down, lay the fleece circle on the back of the picture.

10. Lay a bead of glue around the back of the mat. Press the cardboard square on top, wedging the fleece between the cardboard and the picture. (The fleece puffs out the fabric scene in the mat opening, giving it a rounded look.) Weight down the *edges* (not the center) of the mat until the glue is completely dry. Then, just pop the picture into a frame for unique fabric art.

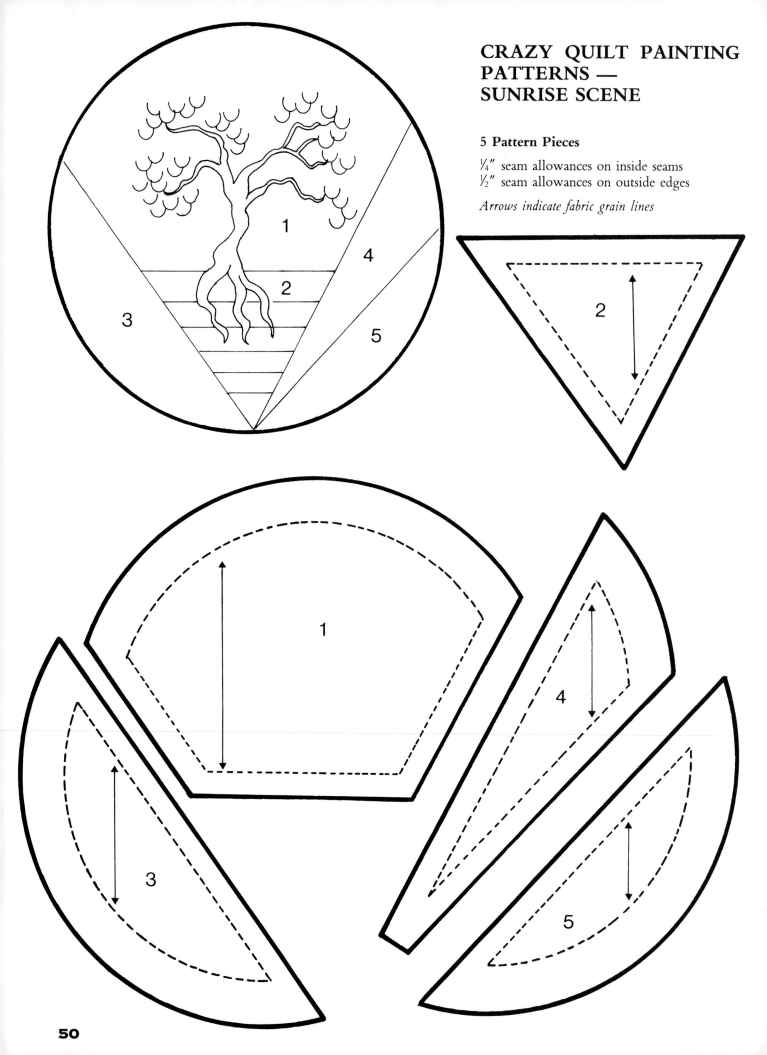

CRAZY QUILT PAINTING PATTERNS — SUNRISE SCENE

5 Pattern Pieces

¼″ seam allowances on inside seams
½″ seam allowances on outside edges

Arrows indicate fabric grain lines

CRAZY QUILT PAINTING PATTERNS — COUNTRY SIDE SCENE

4 Pattern Pieces

¼″ seam allowances on inside seams
½″ seam allowances on outside edges

Arrows indicate fabric grain lines

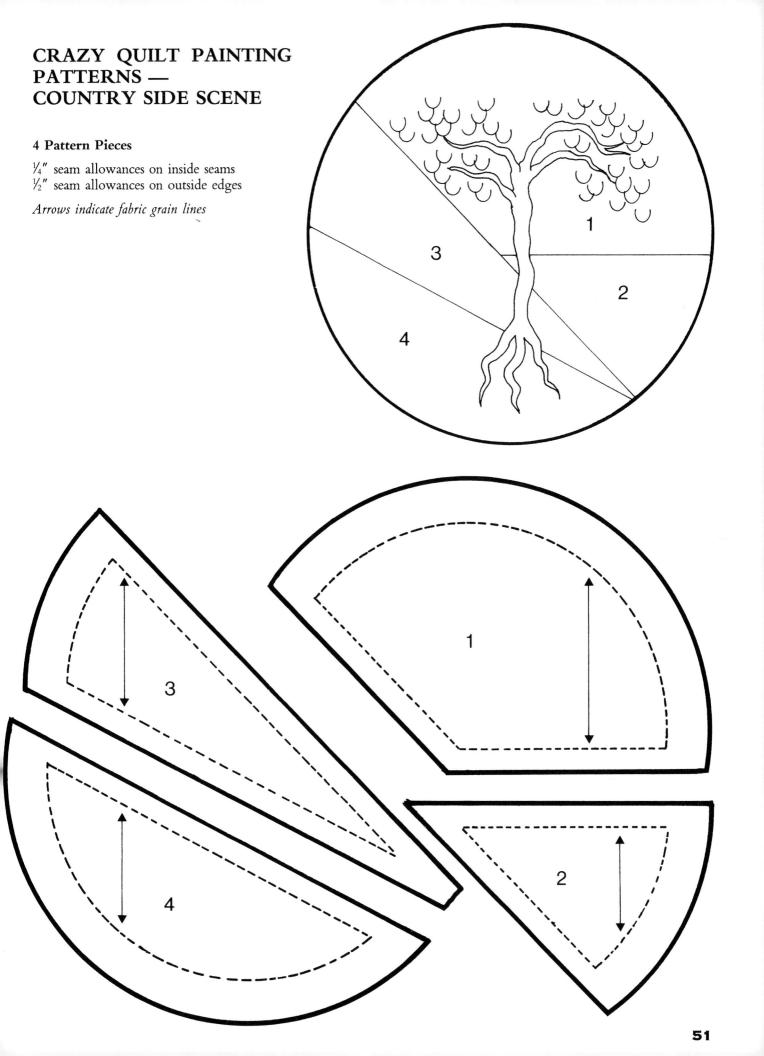

HEART PENDANT

You can make heart pendants in complimentary colors to set off any outfit. When you've made one, chances are you'll want to make more! It's a perfect gift and a beautiful ornament that always attracts notice. it can be made with an embroidery or punchneedle motif of a flower, spider web or free form tree. Embroidered initials make each pendant uniquely personal. Color photos of heart pendants are on Page 41 and on the back cover.

Finished size 3″ × 3¼″

Materials Needed

Fabrics —
> Small scraps of 5-8 fabrics for crazy quilting
> Two 5″ squares of prewashed muslin
> 8″ square dark (black) cotton for embroidered center
> 5″ square leather backing

Other Materials —
> 5″ × 15″ fleece or needlepunch
> 31″ rat-tail cord for neckcord
> 12″ rat-tail cord (another color) for edging
> Fabric glue
> Embroidery floss or silk buttonhole twist
> Darning needle and strong thread
> 5″ square heavy artboard
> Beads, beading needle and nymo thread
> Decorative buttons and/or other trim
> Punchneedle, #1 or #3 (optional)
> Water erasable marker
> Template plastic (optional)

1. Trace the heart shape on Page 53 onto a 4¼″ × 4½″ rectangle of template plastic. With a small scissor or art knife, cut out the heart shape. Use the template to mark the heart shape on your materials. Cut one heart of muslin, three of fleece, one of artboard and one of leather. Do NOT add seam allowances.

2. Trace a flower or some other embroidery design onto the square of dark cotton. First work the outlines of the shape, in either punchneedle or other embroidery, then fill in. If you prefer, you might try fabric painting the design instead of embroidery.

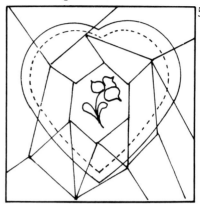

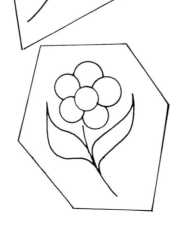

3. Cut out the finished design with enough fabric around it to cut 4-5 angles to start crazy quilting.

4. The remaining muslin square is the base for the crazy quilting. Position the embellished center on it, and begin sewing down small fabric scraps. (See Center Piece Method, Page 16.) Work around, clockwise, until the square is filled in. Press the completed square.

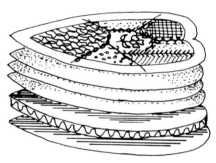

5. Lay the heart template on the crazy quilting and move it around until you find a design placement that you like. Mark the heart shape on the fabric with the water erasable pen. Measure out ½″ all around the heart outline, as illustrated, then cut out the shape on the *outer* line. You need the extra fabric for sewing it to the back.

6. Outline each seam with decorative stitches. (See Stitch Dictionary, Page 65.) Finish off the stitches with beads, French knots or other decorative details.

7. Stack all the cut hearts in order, from the bottom: muslin, artboard, three fleece, and, on top, the crazy quilt heart (this is larger than the others.)

8. With a darning needle and strong thread, whip stitch the crazy quilt heart over the fleece and artboard, using the bottom muslin as an anchor. Sew around twice; on the second round, stitch deeper into the muslin to pull the assembly taut and even.

9. Cut the rat-tail for the neck cord to a length you like. Tie a slip knot at both ends, leaving a ½″ tail.

10. Glue leather backing to heart. Let some glue ooze out of the seam. While the glue is still wet, insert the tails of the neck cord between heart and leather, measuring out ½″ to either side of the heart center (illustrated below). Hold tight until the glue dries.

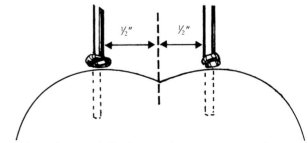

11. Add cord around the heart edges, starting at the center top. (The glue that oozed out will hold it in place.) Whip stitch the cord down with buttonhole twist.

HEART BELT

This belt is made of two crazy quilt hearts, centered on a silk tie-belt. It is most effective and elegant, just the accent you need for a special outfit. The belt ties in the back, so it is adjustable to any waist size. The ends can be tucked in under the belt or left hanging down. The Belt is pictured on Page 41.

Materials Needed

Hearts — See the materials listed for the pendant on Page 52. You need enough to make two hearts. Because there is no neck cord, you need only 12″ of rat-tail to edge each heart.

Belt — ¼ yard silk or comparable fabric
¼ yard cotton (same color as silk)
Matching thread for top stitching
¾ to 1 yard belting or buckram (2¼″ wide)

1. Make two hearts as described on Page 52.

2. Measure your waist. Cut the stiff belting 5″ *shorter* than the waist measurement.

3. Cut the silk and cotton pieces 15″ *longer* than the waist measurement, 5½″ wide.

4. Lay the two fabric pieces together, matching right sides and all edges. On the two *short ends only*, machine stitch ¼″ from the edge. Turn the belt right side out through one of the open sides. This gives you a clean finished end for the tie-belt.

5. Lay the belt flat, cotton side up. Center the belting on top. Now fold the fabric over the belting so that it meets at the center as illustrated below. Whip stitch the fabric edges together by folding one edge over the other. Do not sew through the belting. Finish out to both ends.

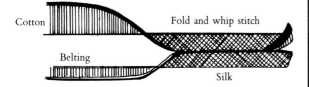

Cotton

Fold and whip stitch

Belting

Silk

6. Machine top stitch through all layers at both edges and the center. Add additional top stitching as desired.

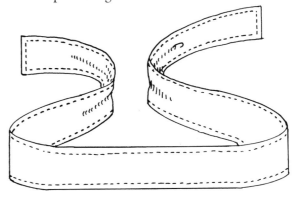

7. Fold the belt in half and mark the center. Glue the hearts in place as illustrated below and in the photo on Page 41. Weigh down the hearts with a heavy book until the glue is completely dry.

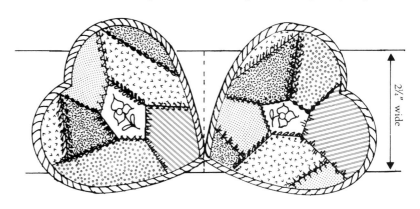

2¼″ wide

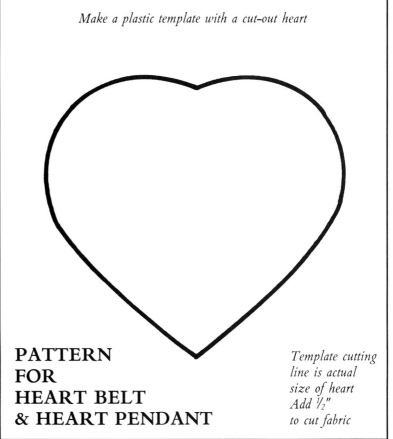

Make a plastic template with a cut-out heart

PATTERN FOR HEART BELT & HEART PENDANT

Template cutting line is actual size of heart Add ½″ to cut fabric

HEART BAG

We often wish we could leave our big purses behind. Here is an elegant answer. This heart bag is just big enough to hold a change purse, lipstick, compact and a small comb. It is pretty enough to double as a large pendant, if desired. It can also be adapted to a belt pocket or needlecase. The technique can be applied to any size or shape of pattern. Refer to the color photo on Page 41.

Finished size 6″ × 6″

Materials Needed

Fabrics —
- Small scraps of 10-12 fancy fabrics
- 9″ square prewashed muslin
- ¼ yard heavy moire or satin for lining, back*

Other Materials —
- 9″ × 16″ fleece or needlepunch
- Embroidery floss or silk buttonhole twist
- Beads, beading needle and nymo thread
- Two pieces (different colors) rat-tail cord, each 45″ long
- 9″ square template plastic (optional)
- Water erasable pen
- Snaps or Velcro circles for closure

*These instructions are for a solid fabric back. If you prefer, you can make a reversible bag by making two crazy quilt hearts.

1. Center a small, angular fabric piece on the muslin square. Using the Center Piece Method (see Page 16), sew on small scraps of fabric, working clockwise, until the square is filled.

2. Position the template plastic over the heart pattern on the opposite page. Trace the outer heart shape onto the plastic. Using small scissors or an art knife, cut out the heart window.

3. Lay the window template on the crazy quilting. Move it around until you find a design placement that you like. Mark the outline of the heart on the fabric with the water erasable pen. Cut away excess fabric on this marked line.

4. Cover each seam with embroidery stitches. (See Stitch Dictionary, Page 65.) Add initials, spiders and webs, flowers or other motifs. Highlight the stitches with beads. Add other embellishments as desired.

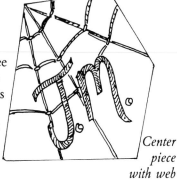

Center piece with web

5. From the lining/backing fabric, cut three hearts, using your window template to mark the shape on the fabric. Cut two hearts of fleece.

6. Put one lining heart on top of the crazy quilted heart, matching right sides and all edges. Place one fleece heart on top, on the back of the lining. Machine stitch all around, taking a ¼″ seam allowance. Leave a 2″ opening on one side as indicated on the pattern.

7. Clip curves and points of the seam allowance, up to the stitching line. Trim fleece to ⅛″ from seam. Turn heart right side out; press it flat. Close the opening by hand.

8. Make the back of the heart bag in the same fashion, using the two remaining hearts of lining/backing and the fleece. When done, you'll have two finished hearts the same size. Press them carefully.

9. Whip stitch the edges of the two hearts together, up to the line designated on the pattern (1½″ from top).

10. Twist the two cord pieces together. Then, decide how you want to put on the cord. It can be adjusted to your desired length one of two ways:

A. Position the center of the cord on your neck or shoulder, letting the cord hang down. At the desired height, pin the cord to both sides of the bag at the point where the two hearts join. Using buttonhole twist, whip the cord to the bag down to the point. Make a small knot in the cord at the point. You can cut away the extra cord or let it dangle loose.

B. Fold the twisted cord in half to find the center. Position the center point of the cord at the bottom point of the heart. Using buttonhole twist, whip the cording onto both sides of the heart up to the point at which back and front separate. Keeping the cords twisted together, tie a knot at the top.

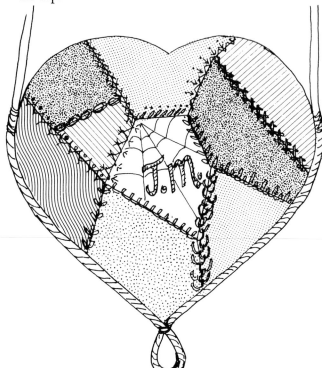

For either method, sew extra wraps around the cord at the top of each side, as illustrated, where it will take the most stress.

HEART BAG PATTERN

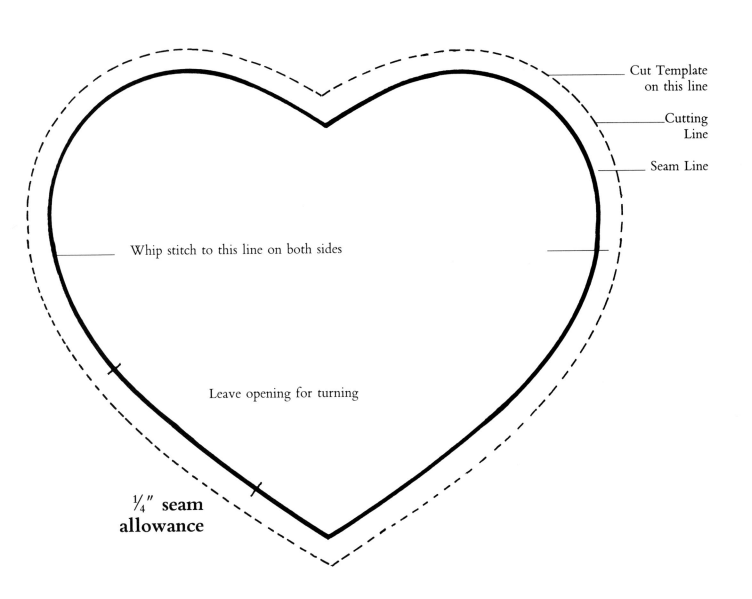

Cut Template on this line

Cutting Line

Seam Line

Whip stitch to this line on both sides

Leave opening for turning

¼″ seam allowance

DESERT MEDALLION

Crazy quilting can be contemporized into unusual fabric scenes like this one. It features a desert scene made from fabric pieces, highlighted with Victorian stitches and beads. It takes on a Western flair with dangling pony beads. (See color photo, Page 40.)

Finished size 4″ round

Materials Needed

Fabrics —
  3¼″ × 6″ sky blue fabric
  Small scraps (desert colors) for scene
  8″ square prewashed muslin
  6″ square leather backing

Other Materials —
  14″ square fleece or needlepunch
  Embroidery floss or silk buttonhold twist
  8″ square heavy artboard
  Water erasable pen
  Fabric glue
  Beads, beading needle and nymo thread
  6″ square template plastic for window, plus extra plastic for pattern pieces
  Darning needle and strong thread
  4-6 pony beads
  50″ each of three different rat-tail cords

1. Center the muslin square on the printed pattern on the facing page. Trace the circle and the design lines onto the muslin.

2. Using the patterns provided, make templates for pieces 3 through 7. The printed patterns include seam allowances — ¼″ on inside seams and ½″ on outside edges. Trace the circle onto the 6″ square of template plastic; cut out circle with a small scissor or art knife.

3. Pieces #1 and #2 are free-form Prairie Points. (To make Prairie Points, see Page 27.) Make Prairie Point #1 from a fabric piece approximately 3¼″ square, and tack down the top point. Fold down a 2¼″ square to make Prairie Point #2. Remember — these Prairie Points will be sewn into a seam, so ¼″ at the bottom edge is for seam allowance.

4. Pin the sky blue fabric on the base, right side up, matching edges at top and side. Pin the Prairie Points in place, extending the bottom edges ¼″ below the marked seam lines.

5. Sew on the remaining pieces in numbered sequence, starting with raw edges and right sides together. Machine stitch through all layers. Press each piece flat before adding the next piece.

6. Center the window template on the finished piece. Mark the 4″ circle on the fabric with water erasable pen. Measure out a ½″ seam allowance all around, then cut away the excess backing fabric.

7. The small plant on the medallion is made of Stem Stitch, with leaves of elongated Lazy Daisies. (See Stitch Dictionary, Page 65.) Add a few French knots, if you like. Finish off the plant with rows of beads. (See Beading, Page 29.) Outline the remaining seams with a variety of embroidery stitches, highlighted with beads.

8. Use your window template to draw 4″ circles on the remaining materials. Cut one circle of muslin, three of fleece and one of artboard. Stack them in that order, with the crazy quilted circle on top. The finished circle should overlap the other circle pieces.

9. With a darning needle and strong thread, whip stitch the finished circle over the fleece and board, using the bottom muslin as an anchor. Sew around twice — on the second round, sew deeper into the bottom muslin to pull the circle taut over the filling.

10. Cut 30″ lengths of the three rat-tail cords. Tie a slip knot at one end, leaving a ½″ tail. Twist the cord until it winds evenly into a pattern, then secure the other end with another slip knot.

11. Find the center at the top of the medallion. Measure out 1″ to either side and mark with a pin.

12. Cut a 4″ circle of leather backing. Glue the leather to the back of the finished medallion circle and hold it tightly in place for several minutes. While the glue is still wet, insert one tail of the knotted cord between the leather and muslin at the point marked by a pin. Retwist the cord and insert the remaining tail. Let a little glue ooze out of the seam.

13. Take the remaining cords and twist them together very tightly. Now tie the cord around the outside of the medallion and knot it on the bottom with a slip knot. You should feel it slip into place on the edge. Some of the glue that oozed out will help anchor the cord in place. Finish off the dangling ends with pony beads, and knot each cord so the bead won't slip off.

PATTERNS FOR DESERT MEDALLION

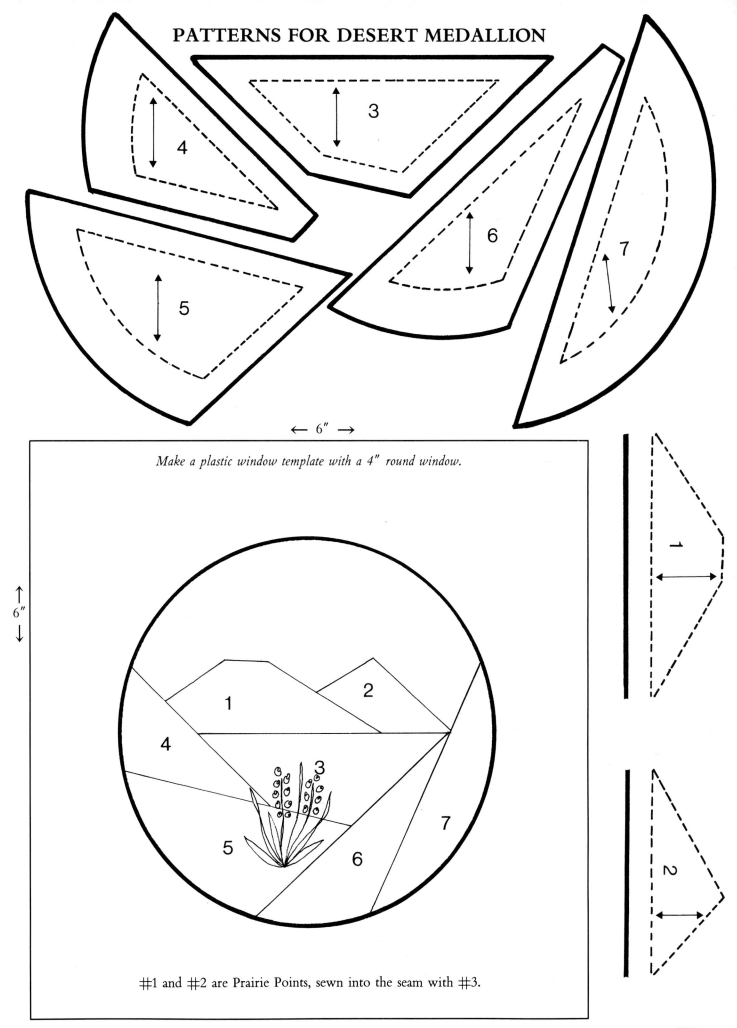

← 6" →

Make a plastic window template with a 4" round window.

6"

#1 and #2 are Prairie Points, sewn into the seam with #3.

58A. *A variety of frame and mat styles show the versatility of crazy quilt paintings. Embroidery and beads create different effects. The outstanding cactus button shown at left adds dimension to the picture.*

58B. *The desert wears colors both blazing and subtle, from deep purple to brilliant blue. This picture is worked in deep shades of rust and blue, highlighted with a cactus button. Shown courtesy of Pat Rogers.*

58C. *This tree pendant is a variation of the Desert Medallion project given on Page 56. Use those instructions to create a medallion of your own design. Shown courtesy of Carol Moderi.*

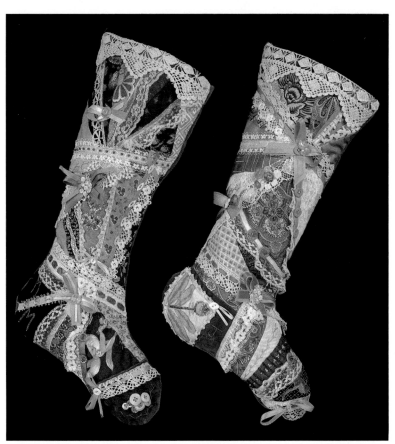

59B. Crazy quilt jackets dress up two Teddy bears. The jackets are made of crazy quilted rectangles, cut and shaped to be bear wear. Doll made by Elinor Peace Bailey.

59A. Crazy quilt stockings, hung by the chimney with care, are just the touch to remind us of the Victorian Christmases Dickens must have known. Lavishly detailed with lace, ribbon and buttons, they can be personalized with initials or names.

59C. A blessed event is recorded in this framed christening keepsake, highlighted with lace, ribbon and calligraphy. Courtesy of Melissa Brinkman.

OVAL BELT BUCKLES

When is a belt buckle not a belt buckle? The answer is when it's a medallion attached to a tie belt. These oval "buckles" are really wonderful because they are attached with Velcro and can be interchanged to suit different outfits. So, all you need is one tie-belt and several different buckles. Three buckle designs are shown, but really the sky is the limit on this project. Experiment to come up with your own design. (See color photo, Page 41.)

Finished size 3″ × 4½″

Materials Needed

Fabrics for buckle —
    Small scraps of 6-8 fancy fabrics
       (include sky blue for picture buckles)
    Two 6″ squares prewashed muslin
    6″ square leather backing

Fabrics for belt —
    ¼ yard dark (black) silk or comparable fabric
    ¼ yard cotton (same color)
    ¾ to 1 yard for belting, 2″ wide

Other materials for buckle —
    6″ × 14″ fleece or needlepunch
    Embroidery floss or silk buttonhole twist
    Silver metallic thread for spider web (optional)
    Beads, beading needle and nymo thread
    Darning needle and strong thread
    6″ square artboard
    15″ rat-tail cord
    5″ × 7″ rectangle template plastic for window
    Extra plastic for pattern templates (optional)
    3″ strip Velcro
    Fabric glue
    Water erasable pen
    Matching thread for belt topstitching

General Instructions

1. Instructions for making the tie belt are given on Page 53. This belt, however, should be only 2″ wide. Cut the silk and cotton strips 5″ wide, then proceed with the belt instructions as given.

2. Make a plastic template for the oval, using the pattern given on the opposite page. Use the template to mark the oval on the other materials. Cut one oval of muslin, three of fleece, one of artboard and one of leather.

3. Select the design you wish to make from the three given here, or create one of your own. Instructions for each option are given below. Follow those instructions to fill in the remaining muslin square.

4. Use the oval template to mark the design area on the crazy quilting. Add ½″ seam allowances all around, and cut out the oval.

5. Outline each seam with embroidery stitches. Highlight the stitches with beads.

6. Stack all the ovals together, with the muslin oval on the bottom, then the artboard, three fleece, and the crazy quilted oval on top. The crazy quilted oval will be larger than the others.

7. With the darning needle and heavy-duty thread, whip stitch the crazy quilted oval over the fleece and board, using the bottom muslin as an anchor. Sew around twice — on the second round, stitch deeper into the muslin to pull the assembly taut and even.

8. Glue leather to the back of the oval, and apply the leather backing. Hold the leather in place for several minutes to let the glue set. It's okay if a little bit of glue oozes out of the seam (it will help hold the cord in place).

9. Whip the rat-tail cord around the outer edge of the oval with buttonhole twist.

10. Glue the Velcro strip to the back of the buckle, lengthwise as illustrated at right, making sure it is centered. Sew the opposite side of the Velcro at the center of the tie belt.

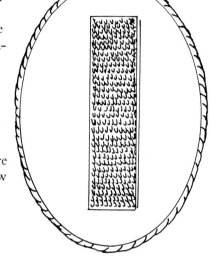

SANTA FE BUCKLE

1. This buckle is put together just like the crazy quilt paintings and the desert medallion. Pieces A, B and C are free-form prairie points, the rest are pattern pieces. Sew the pieces directly onto the marked muslin square, working in the numbered sequence shown.

2. Press carefully to make the prairie points lay flat. Then, lay down the window template and mark the design area. Add ½″ seam allowances all around and cut out the oval. Complete the buckle according the general instructions.

SEA SCAPE BUCKLE

1. The Sea Scape buckle is a challenge pattern. Either make your own patterns from the fullsize drawing given, or cut the fabric free-form as you sew. The drawing shows the numerical sequence in which the fabrics are sewn onto the marked muslin square.

2. If you choose to work free-form, refer to the How-To section (Page 15) for guidelines. If you decide to make patterns, be sure all inside seam allowances are ¼″ and all the outside edges have ½″ seam allowances. The extra on the outside gives you enough fabric to whip stitch over the fleece and artboard.

3. Refer to the Stitch Dictionary for tips on making free-form trees (Page 79).

SPIDER WEB BUCKLE

1. On your muslin square, center a small dark fabric piece that has four or five angles. Now, using the Center Piece Method described on Page 16, sew down irregular pieces of fabric. Work around clockwise until the square is filled.
2. Use your window template to find and mark a pleasing design area.
3. Refer to the Stitch Dictionary for details on spiders and webs (Page 79). Work a web on the center dark fabric. (Silver metallic thread makes an especially glittery web). Embellish the rest of the oval as desired, then proceed with the buckle instructions as given.

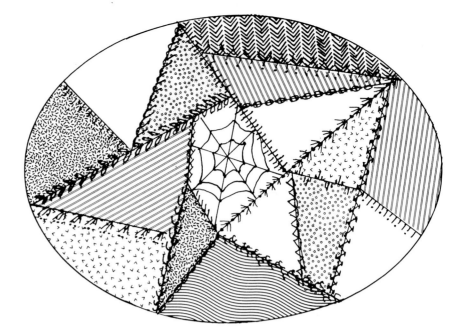

Santa Fe Buckle Patterns are on Page 64.

PLASTIC WINDOW TEMPLATE

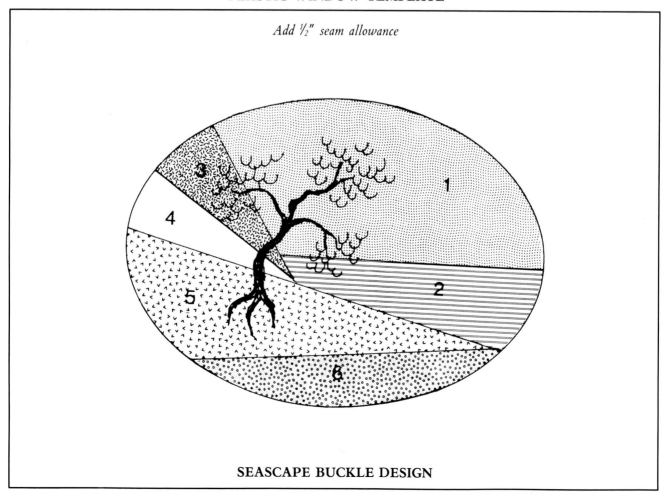

Add ½" seam allowance

SEASCAPE BUCKLE DESIGN

62A. This T-dress is made of black wool challis with complementary cuffs. The front panel of crazy quilting features punchneedle and silk embroidery. Shown courtesy of Lola Meagher.

62B. This T-dress, with crazy quilt yolk, cuffs and hem, is made of cotton and cotton blends by Concord. Shown courtesy of Priscilla Miller.

63A. A commercial pattern by Folkwear (see Source List) is the basis for "Dance of the Ghosts," a contemporary crazy quilt design incorporating the deserts and mountains of the American Indians. Made with silks, cottons and silk embroideries, this garment was made for a special show, Cut From the Same Cloth, mounted by Marinda Brown-Stewart.

63B. Old ties are the primary ingredient in this all-over crazy quilt vest.

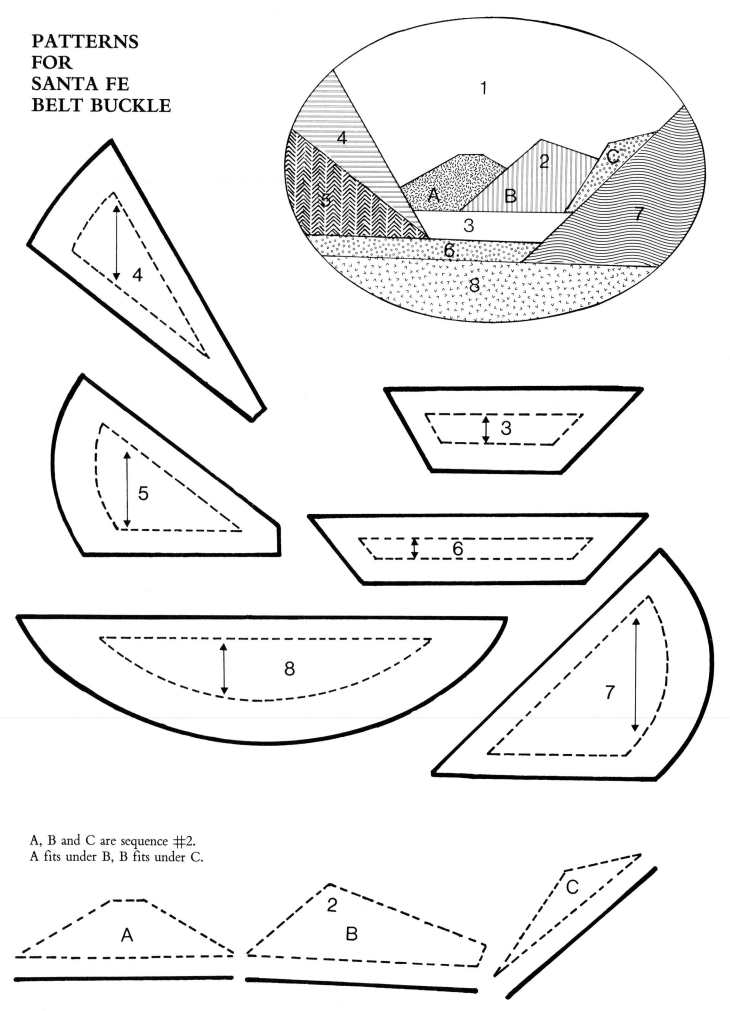

PATTERNS
FOR
SANTA FE
BELT BUCKLE

A, B and C are sequence #2.
A fits under B, B fits under C.

Stitch Dictionary

This is a dictionary of 16 stitches and motifs commonly used in crazy quilting. For each, there is a step-by-step illustration and a photograph of the finished stitch. Once you have mastered the basics, you can go on to the variations shown. Most often, embroidery stitches are used to cover seam lines on the base work, but they can also be used as decorative elements anywhere on the piece. Combined with ribbon, beads and other embellishments, they make crazy quilting come alive.

"Adding Other Stitches" shows how to combine stitches. Combinations of stitches work well in crazy quilting because they add so much color and design. By using different colored thread for each step, you can create wonderful highlights in your work. Try the combinations illustrated, then strike out on your own. Remember that repetition of stitches is an important element in good design.

Many students get upset if their stitches are not perfect the first time around. Like most skills, good embroidery stitching requires practice. To begin with, just remember that consistency and repetition of the stitch is the design maker. If the stitches are too wide, keep them wide and persevere. If the stitches are too small, too short, or uneven, keep repeating and you will come up with a design stitch all your own. As you practice, you'll find you can control the stitching better and it will become easier.

A Special Note

Silk buttonhole twist works beautifully for Victorian stitches. I don't use anything else for seam stitches. It comes in a variety of vibrant colors and gives a beautiful sheen to the stitches. The silk slides very smoothly through the fabric. Silk buttonhole twist can be found in better fabric stores, usually in 10 yard lengths wrapped on wooden spools. There are other silk twisted threads that also work well, some from Japan and Europe. Japanese silk is usually wrapped on a cardboard disk.

STRAIGHT STITCH

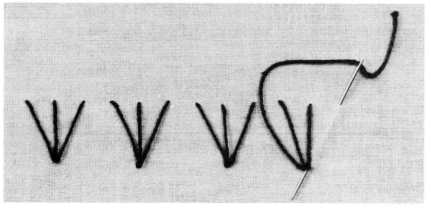

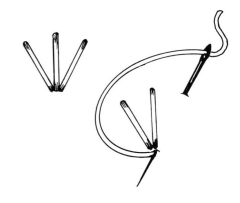

Straight stitches can be used in a variety of ways. Long or short, they should not be too loose, so pull threads firmly into place.

COUCHING

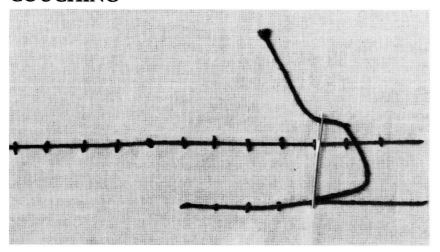

This is a decorative way to hold long threads in place. Lay down long threads as desired. Now, with either matching or contrasting thread, come up at regular intervals and wrap a small, tight stitch over the long thread.

FRENCH KNOTS

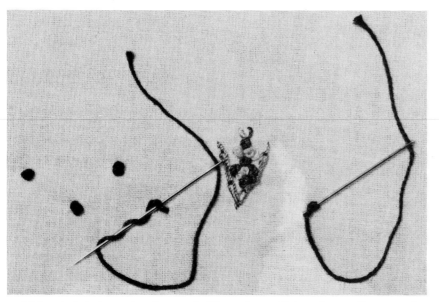

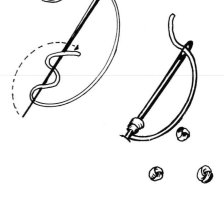

This stitch is just what it sounds like, a knot. Bring the needle up and circle the needle twice around the thread. Hold the thread taut as you twist the needle over and under the thread, and as you insert the needle back into the fabric, as close as possible to the starting point. Hold the knot in place until the needle has passed through it. For extra security, secure the knot in the back.

BUTTONHOLE STITCH

This stitch is worked from left to right. Hold the thread down with your thumb and make a downward vertical stitch. Bring the needle over the thread and pull into place. The bottom line formed should lie on the seam line. Make sure the vertical stitches are straight and even.

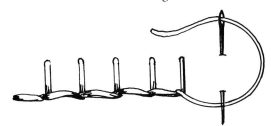

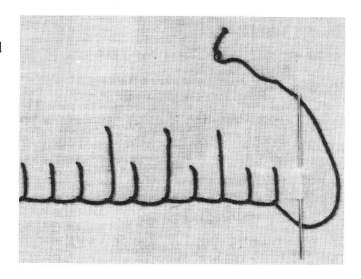

VARIATIONS

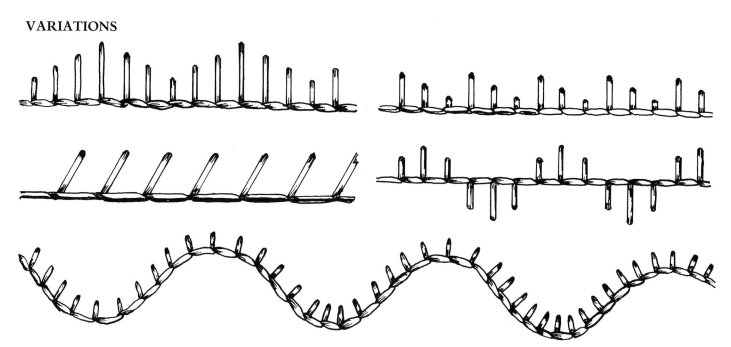

ADDING OTHER STITCHES

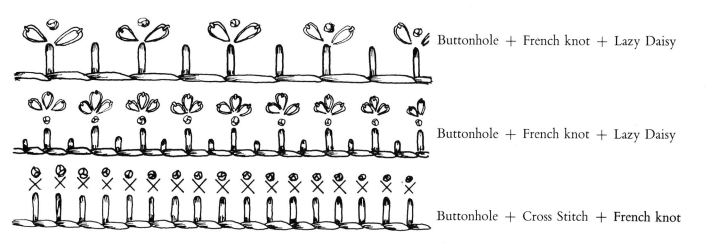

Buttonhole + French knot + Lazy Daisy

Buttonhole + French knot + Lazy Daisy

Buttonhole + Cross Stitch + French knot

SATIN STITCH

Satin Stitch was a favorite of Victorian crazy quilters. It can be worked in single or double layers to create a thick, smooth blanket of stitching. The stitch can be worked straight up and down, side to side, or at an angle, laying down straight stitches close together to conform to the outlined shape. The photos below are examples of satin stitch taken from several antique crazy quilts.

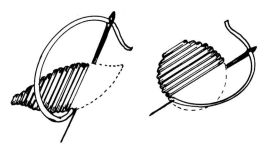

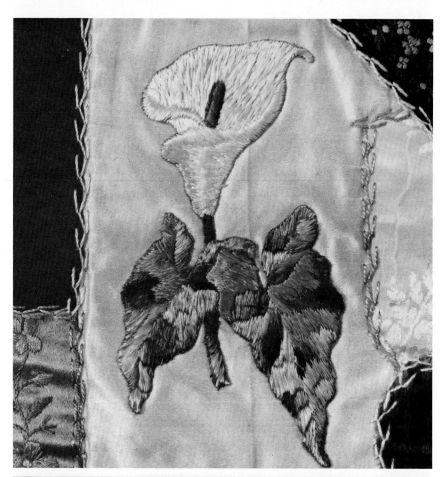

Flowers, initials and other shapes acquire depth and texture in Satin Stitch. The peacock at left is worked in Long & Short, a variation of Satin Stitch that alternates different stitch lengths.

HERRINGBONE STITCH

The herringbone stitch is worked from left to right and lies evenly on both sides of the seam. It is created by taking a small horizontal back stitch on each side of the seam. Be sure to keep the horizontal stitches even as this creates the design.

VARIATIONS

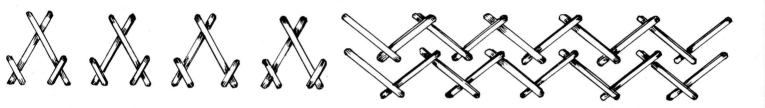

ADDING OTHER STITCHES

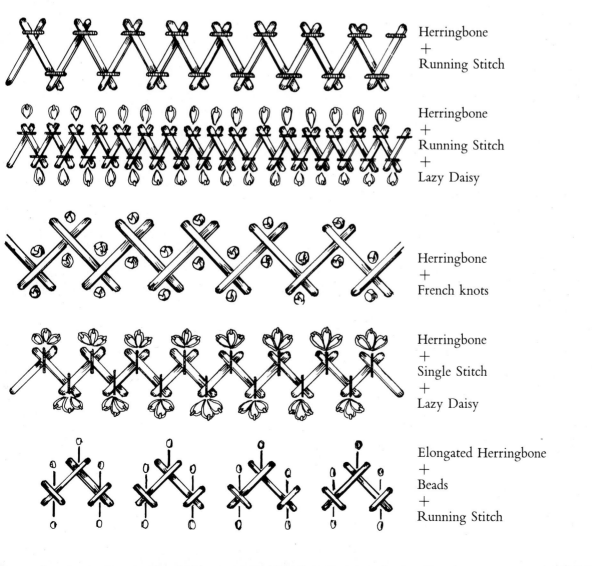

Herringbone
+
Running Stitch

Herringbone
+
Running Stitch
+
Lazy Daisy

Herringbone
+
French knots

Herringbone
+
Single Stitch
+
Lazy Daisy

Elongated Herringbone
+
Beads
+
Running Stitch

FEATHER STITCH

This stitch begins with a single feather stitch and alternates back and forth. The feather stitch is a vertical stitch and is worked down towards you. The only secret to this stitch is to remember to always put the needle in at B, straight across from where the thread came out at A.

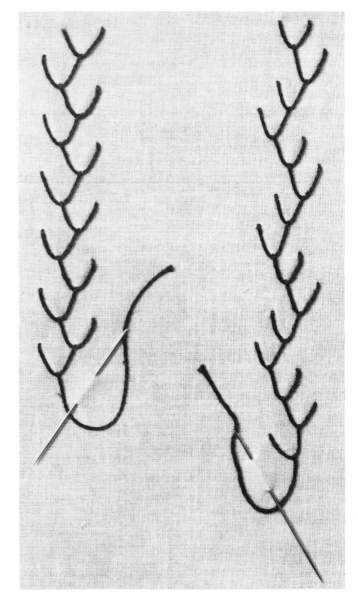

ADDING OTHER STITCHES

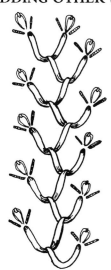

Feather Stitch
+
Lazy Daisy
+
Straight Stitch

Feather Stitch
+
Beads

Feather Stitch
+
Lazy Daisy
+
French knot

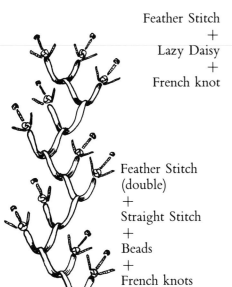

Feather Stitch
(double)
+
Straight Stitch
+
Beads
+
French knots

VARIATIONS

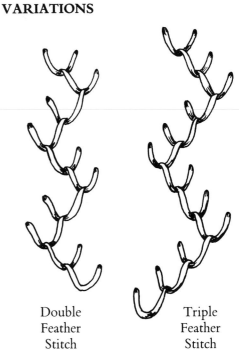

Double
Feather
Stitch

Triple
Feather
Stitch

CHEVRON STITCH

This is another stitch that lies horizontally and evenly on each side of a seam. It is worked left to right. Start in the lower corner and take a short stitch forward, then a half stitch back. Work the same stitch on the upper line just a little to the right. Work this stitch alternately from one side to the other. Be sure to keep the small backstitches evenly spaced.

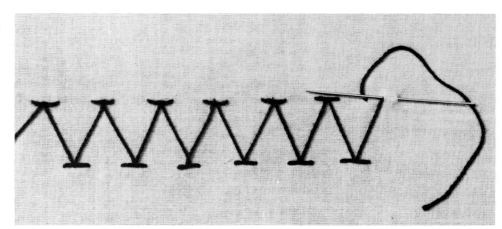

VARIATIONS

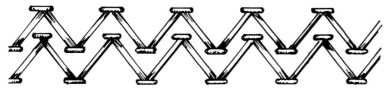

ADDING OTHER STITCHES

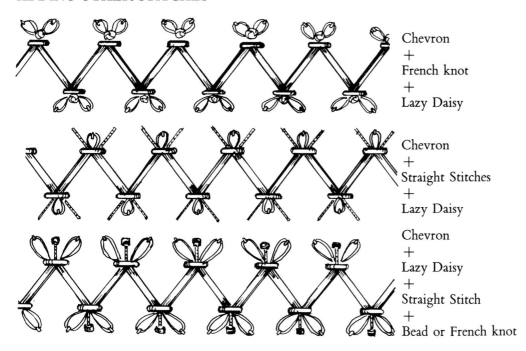

Chevron
+
French knot
+
Lazy Daisy

Chevron
+
Straight Stitches
+
Lazy Daisy

Chevron
+
Lazy Daisy
+
Straight Stitch
+
Bead or French knot

CRETAN STITCH

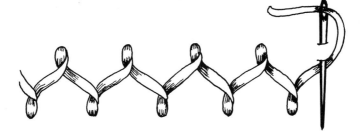

The cretan stitch starts in the bottom left corner and is worked from left to right. Short vertical stitches are worked alternately downward and upward. Hold the thread down so the needle will pass over it. This stitch should be worked evenly on each side of a seam. Be sure to keep the vertical stitches even.

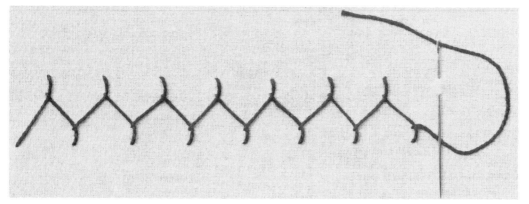

VARIATIONS

ADDING OTHER STITCHES

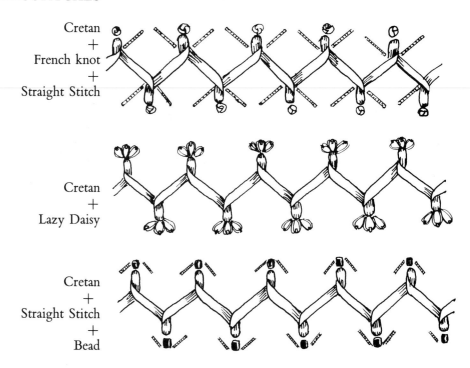

Cretan
+
French knot
+
Straight Stitch

Cretan
+
Lazy Daisy

Cretan
+
Straight Stitch
+
Bead

LAZY DAISY STITCH

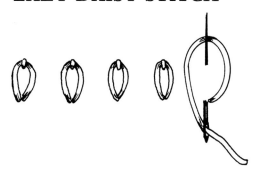

The lazy daisy is a looped stitch, like a free-floating chain stitch. It can be worked in rows or used randomly. Bring the thread up through the fabric. Hold it down with your thumb and insert the needle again at the starting point. Bring it out a short distance away, making sure the needle comes over the thread. Now take a small holding stitch at the top of the loop.

VARIATIONS

ADDING OTHER STITCHES

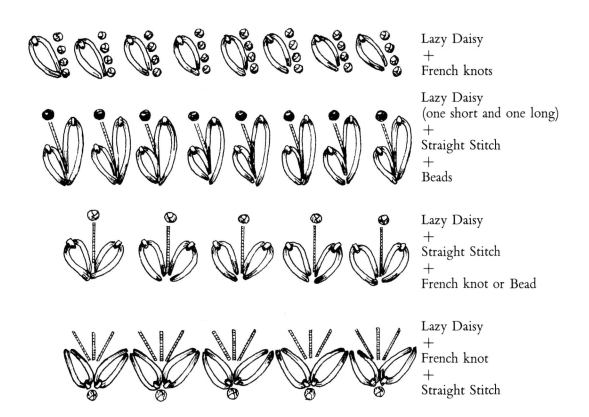

Lazy Daisy
+
French knots

Lazy Daisy
(one short and one long)
+
Straight Stitch
+
Beads

Lazy Daisy
+
Straight Stitch
+
French knot or Bead

Lazy Daisy
+
French knot
+
Straight Stitch

CHAIN STITCH

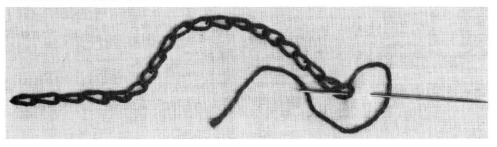

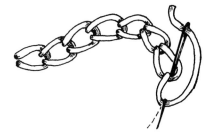

The Chain Stitch is similar to the Lazy Daisy except that it is continuous. Pull up the thread at the starting point and hold it down with your finger. Bring the needle down into the starting point and come up again a short distance away. Be sure the needle comes up *over* the thread, forming a loop. Repeat to make a chain.

RUNNING STITCH

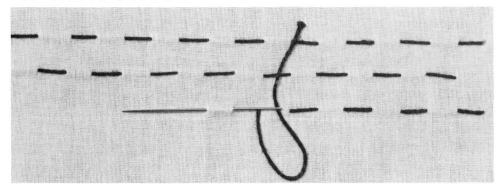

The Running Stitch is worked from right to left. Make small, even stitches. The stitch that shows should be the same width as the spaces.

STEM STITCH

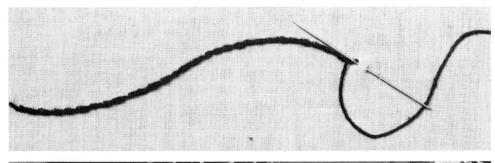

The Stem Stitch works from left to right. Sew along the stitch line and keep the thread to the left of the needle. Take small, even stitches. When laying stitch lines side by side to fill in an area, be sure to fit them snugly in order to cover.

Detail from Baker quilt, pictured on Page 22. Bessie Baker used Stem Stitch, with satin stitch, to embroider her initials on her 1930's crazy quilt.

CROSS STITCH

The first step is to make a row of even diagonal stitches, working from lower right to upper left, working across to the left. Next, work back to the right with another diagonal line overlaying the first that goes from bottom left to upper right to form an X. This stitch should lie evenly over a seam.

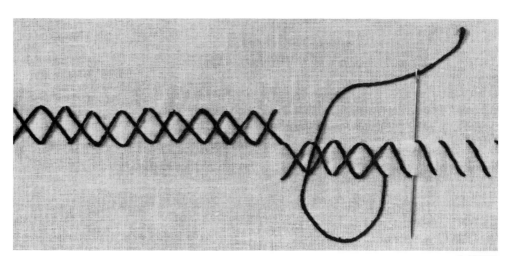

CLOSED BUTTONHOLE

This stitch is similar to the regular buttonhole, except that two vertical stitches are worked into the same hole. This forms the triangle shapes.

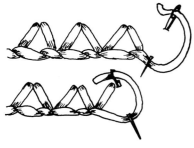

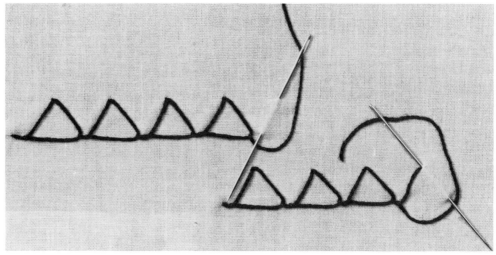

VARIATIONS

ADDING OTHER STITCHES

Closed Buttonhole + French knot + Fans

FANS

Embroidered fans are a traditional decorative touch in crazy quilting. They are very effective used in a row to cover seam lines or enlarged to act as a highlight. Be sure to pull the threads firmly into place. Otherwise they will snag and lose their shape.

COMBINING STITCHES

Straight Stitches + Running Stitches

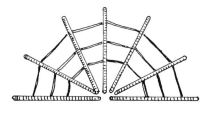

Straight Stitches + Cross Stitches

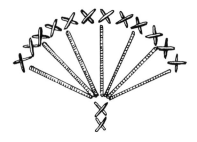

Straight Stitches + Beads + Lazy Daisy

Stem Stitches + Running Stitch + French knot

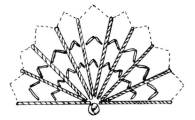

Straight Lines + French knots

VARIATIONS

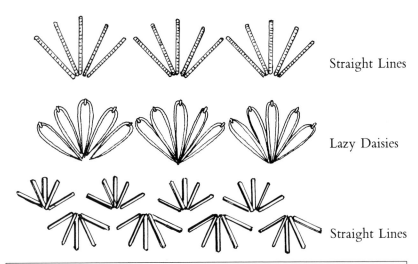

Straight Lines

Lazy Daisies

Straight Lines

Fans are also a favorite motif in fabric. Pieced fans are great fillers, eye catchers and really fun to make! They are marvelous backgrounds for stitches, too. Refer to Page 17 for more tips on using pieced fans.

WEBS

What is a crazy quilt without a spider and its web? This is a favorite embroidery motif. Metallic and iridescent threads make them terrific. A good quality of metallic thread will not unravel. Using short threads will help prevent the unravelling problem, too. Some metallics are wrapped around a thread core and will break away if used too roughly. All spokes of the webs shown are couched down. Try using a smooth, spun metallic thread for the couching stitches.

FOUR INTERSECTING SPOKES

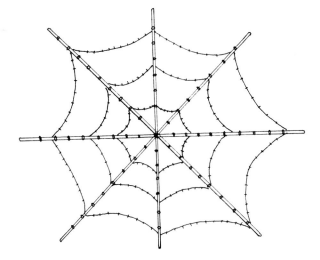

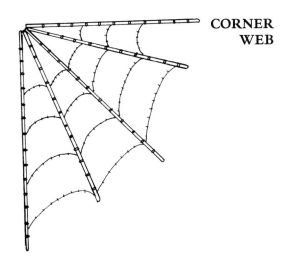

CORNER WEB

6-SPOKE WEB WITH CONTINUOUS THREAD

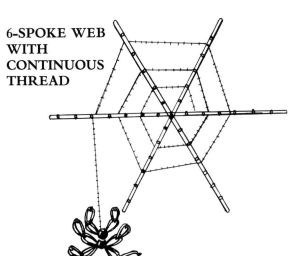

SPIDERS

Spiders are a unique, very traditional part of crazy quilting. In Europe, they are considered good luck when worked into needlework. But it can be difficult to make them look nice. My compromise is to make them with six legs instead of eight. Each leg is made of two chain stitches, connected to a body made of two iridescent beads.

FREE-FORM TREES

This is a good example of experimenting with and combining stitches. The tree I use most is made of Feather Stitch, Stem and Chain Stitches (see Medallion, Photo 58C). The trunk and branches are Stem and Chain, laid closely together to act as fillers and to give the illusion of a bark-like texture. A variety of colors creates shading. The Feather stitches are random, to represent leaves and twigs. Make the Feather stitches uneven and free. Adding beads creates further highlights.

Combining other stitches can create different kinds of trees. The examples below show combinations of Lazy Daisy, Satin and Straight stitches that create trees with widely different "personalities." Willow, bonsai, apple and other types of trees can be wonderful highlights in crazy quilting.

BIBLIOGRAPHY

Aikman, Susanne Z.
A Primer: The Art of Native American Beadwork
1980, Morning Flower Press, Denver, CO

Bond, Dorothy
Crazy Quilt Stitches
1981, Self Published, Cottage Grove, OR

Brown-Stewart, Marinda
Ideas & Inspirations, A Punchneedle Techniques Primer
Self Published, El Cerrito, CA

Coats & Clark
100 Embroidery Stitches
1964, Coats & Clark, New York, NY

Conroy, Mary
300 Years of Canada's Quilts
1976, Griffin House, Toronto, Ontario

Dorling Kindersley Ltd.
The Pattern Library, Embroidery
1981, Ballentine Books, New York, NY

Gross, Joyce
Quilters Journal, Vol. 1, #3, #5, #6
Self Published, P.O. Box 270, Mill Valley, CA 94941

Haywood, Dixie
Crazy Quilting with a Difference
1981, Dover Publications, Inc., New York, NY

Horton, Roberta
Calico and Beyond
1986, C&T Publishing, Lafayette, CA

Laury, Jean Ray
New Uses for Old Laces
1974, Doubleday & Co., Garden City, NY
Quilts and Coverlets
1970, Van Nostrand Reinhold Co., New York, NY

Lyford, Carrie A.
Quill and Beadwork of the Western Sioux
1979, Johnson Publishing Co., Boulder, CO

McMorris, Penny
Crazy Quilts
1984, E.P. Dutton, New York, NY

Meilach, Dona Z. and Menagh, Dee
Exotic Needlework
1978, Crown Publishers, Inc., New York, NY

Nichols, Marion
Encyclopedia of Embroidery Stitches, Including Crewel
1974, Dover Publications, New York, NY

Pucket, Marjorie and Giberson, Gail
Primarily Patchwork
1975, Cabin Craft, Redlands, CA

Vanessa Ann Collection, The
In Times Past
1982, Ogden, UT

Wells, Jean
A Patchworthy Apparel Book
1981, Yours Truly, Inc., Westminster, CA

Wilson, Erica
Crewel Embroidery
1982, Chas. Scribner's Sons, New York, NY
The Craft of Silk and Gold Thread Embroidery and Stump Work
1973, Chas. Scribner's Sons, New York, NY

SOURCE LIST

Aardvark Adventures in Handcrafts
P.O. Box 2449, Livermore, CA 94550
Natesh threads, metallics, stamps, buttons, beads
Also has a wonderful newspaper that acts as a catalog and information source; send stamps (37¢) and return address.

Birdhouse Enterprises
110 Jennings Ave., Dept. JM, Patchogue, NY 11772
Punchneedles in three sizes, gauges, special hoops, and instruction books
Send SASE* for free catalog. Will ship to Canada with U.S. money order and $1.00 additional postage.

Marinda Brown-Stewart
P.O. Box 402, Dept. J, Walnut Creek, CA 94596
T-Dress pattern, punchneedle books, painted fabrics
Send SASE* for free catalog. Will ship to Canada.

Fashion Blueprints
2191 Blossom Valley Dr., San Jose, CA 95124
Ethnic patterns with craft ideas
Send $1.00 for catalog. Will ship to Canada.

Folkware Patterns
Customer Service, Dept. CQ, Tanton Press, Box 5506, Newton, CT 06470-5506
Authentic ethnic and antique garment patterns
Send $2.00 for catalog.

Western Trading Post
P.O. Box 9070, Denver, CO 80209-0070
Beads, beading needles, feathers, beading thread, books, etc.
Send $3.00 for catalog. Will ship to Canada.

Clarke's O Sew Easy Punch Embroidery
252 Vega Drive, Goleta, CA 93117
Punchneedles, patterns, kits, and yarns for all punch embroidery
Retail and Wholesale catalog. Will ship to Canada.

Anne's Glory Box
625 Hunter Street, New Castle West, N.S.W., Australia 2302
Complete line of quilting, embroidery, and other needlework supplies
Retail and Wholesale catalog. Send business size SASE*.

The Cotton Patch
1025 Brown Ave., Lafayette, CA 94549
A complete quilting supply store featuring over 750 solid cotton fabrics
Send $3.00 for catalog and fabric swatches. Will ship worldwide.

Bernina of America
534 West Chestnut
Hinsdale, IL 60521
Judith uses and recommends Bernina machines.
Free brochures on all Berninas, Bernette sergers, and assorted sewing equipment.

Treadleart
25834 Narbonne Ave., Lomita, CA 90717
Embroidery supplies, books, fabrics, and sewing gadgets
Send $2.00 for catalog. Will ship worldwide.

Judith Designs
P.O. Box 177, Castle Rock, CO 80104
Findings from around the world for crazy quilting and clothing embellishment: doodads, fabric kits, beads, buttons, silk thread and ribbon
Send $1.50 for catalog. Will ship worldwide.

Grandma Graphics
Dept. BCQ, 20 Birling Gap, Fairport, NY 14450-3916
Photo sun print kits
Send SASE* for free price list. Will ship to Canada.

The Hands Work
P.O. Box 386, Pecos, NM 87552
Handmade and handpainted machine washable buttons
Send $2.00 (refundable with first order) for catalog. Will ship to Canada.

Maiden Vermont Buttons, Danforth Pewterers
P.O. Box 828, Middlebury, VT 05753
Buttons in many shapes: animals, flowers, moons, hearts, quilt patterns, sea shells, etc. Also pewter buttons, pins and jewelry in many shapes.
For free catalog call 1-800-222-5260. Will ship to Canada.

Yvonne Porcella Studios
3619 Shoemaker, Modesto, CA 95351
Pieced clothing, pieced clothing variations, jacket patterns
Send SASE* for free catalog. Will ship to Canada.

Thai Silks
252 State Street, Los Altos, CA 94022
Silk, cotton and wool fabrics, the largest selection of silk yardage in the U.S.
Send SASE* for free information. Will ship to Canada.

Y.L.I. Corporation
45 West 300 North, Provo, UT 84601
Kanagawa silk threads and ribbons from Tokyo. Over 100 colors, different weights, metallic threads. Other needlework supplies. Judith uses this thread exclusively in her work.
Retail and Wholesale catalog. Will ship to Canada.

Quilter's Helper
P.O. Box 519, 5511 Main St., Osgoode, Ontario, Canada KOA-2WO
Specialized cottons for quilting and home decorating, books, and supplies
Send $3.00 for catalog and fabric swatches.

*Self-addressed stamped envelope